DESIGN PORTFOLIOS OF THE

ELEGANT EAST

Eric Tai

SendPoints

DESIGN PORTFOLIOS OF THE

ELEGANT EAST

First printing of the first edition, November 2020

SendPoints

PUBLISHED BY SendPoints IPS Co., Ltd.
EDITED BY Metto International Ltd.
PUBLISHER: Lin Gengli
PUBLISHING DIRECTOR: Zhai Dongxiao
CHIEF EDITOR: Eric Tai
DESIGN DIRECTOR: Liu Jinghua

REGISTERED ADDRESS: Flat/Rm 4,5/F, Tak Lee Building, 270-280 Queens Road West Hongkong
TEL: +852 6950 2452 / **FAX:** +852 3583 2448
OFFICE ADDRESS: 7F, No.9-1 Anning Street, Jinshazhou Road, Baiyun District, Guangzhou, China
TEL: +86-20-89095121 / **FAX:** +86-20-89095206
BEIJING OFFICE: Room 513, 5th Floor, Building 1, Longde Zijinjia, No.186 Litang Road, Changping District, Beijing, China
TEL: +86-10-84139071 / **FAX:** +86-10-84139071
SHANGHAI OFFICE: Room 302, Floor 3, Ningbo Road no.349, Huangpu District, Shanghai, China
TEL: +86-21-63523469 / **FAX:** +86-21-63523469

ISBN 978-988-74068-4-6

Printed and bound in China.

Eric Tai, founder and Chief Creative Officer of Eric Tai design brand. Mr Tai served as a special lecturer in the advanced research class of Academy of Arts & Design at Tsinghua University. He was selected as China's Top Ten Designers and his work was elected to Andrew Martin International Design Award. He has published a lot of works, such as *Neo-Chinese Elegance*, *Fusion*, and *Chinese Style Elegance*.

PREFACE

/Eric Tai

It has been four years since my last work was published, and I was engaged in a couple of projects and underprepared for new book. Given that COVID-19 pandemic has spread worldwide, this year was quite special. All of a sudden, life and work pace slowed down, and bought me some time to look back on my works over the years.

When looking back to those works, memories were still so close to me from meeting customers' needs, managing details to showing final design. Each project witnessed standardized and strict creation process. I moved forward with hope, and overcame difficulties constantly as well as occasional burnout. The more new projects the more responsibilities I take over. It came to me as a relief everytime I complete a project.

This book *The Elegant East* was regarded as a collection of works, of which 29 selected works were typical projects that were customized in accordance with different needs, showcasing unique charms. Due to page limitation, many projects failed to be selected. Yet, they are available on the Internet. In order to avoid being bulky, we chose slightly thinner sheets to provide readers with better reading experience. In the era of Internet, e-reading is the trend in the future, and p-books are more intended for collection. No matter in which forms, we hope more people can enjoy the joy of reading.

This book, together with *Chinese Style Elegance*, *Fusion and Neo-Chinese Elegance*, has become a serie of design books that constantly summarize and improve interior aesthetics and enable a systematic understanding of the elegance in Eastern design. For interior designer, the pursuit of creating beauty out of space meanwhile inspire more aesthetical practise to discover the beauty of life really means a lot.

We thank all the readers for your long-term confidence and support so that we can publish this book with creativity. We thank all the members of Eric Tai design team for your joint efforts and companionships. We thank all the participated units. We thank Chen Weizhong, Chen Yanming, Chen Jianzhong and Zhao Hongfei for your photography. We thank graphic designer Liu Jinghua for book design. And we thank publisher Mr. Zhai Dongxiao.

May 7, 2020 in Shenzhen

CONTENTS

Project:
Sales Center of Jiangshanzhu

Client:
Kunda Group

Location:
Zhengzhou

Stream and Mountain

Stream and mountain are inspired by a poem written by Su Shi, a renowned Chinese poet in Song Dynasty. The poem was a gift to Chang Zong in Donglin Temple. As the poem goes, the sound of flowing stream is as eloquent as Buddha's sermon, from which you learn everything, and blue sky and white clouds represent legal bodies of purity. The building of sales center adopts "mountain" as creation element, and inherits elegant and decorous building style with development and abstraction, creating an interior style of "outward prosperity and inward quietness" as well as an Eastern vibe of peace and implication.

Main materials: Sliver Blossom; Milan Grey Marble; Landscape Purple Marble; Tile; Oak; Art Glass
Area: 1,300 m^2
Design Time: July 2018
Completion Time: August 2019

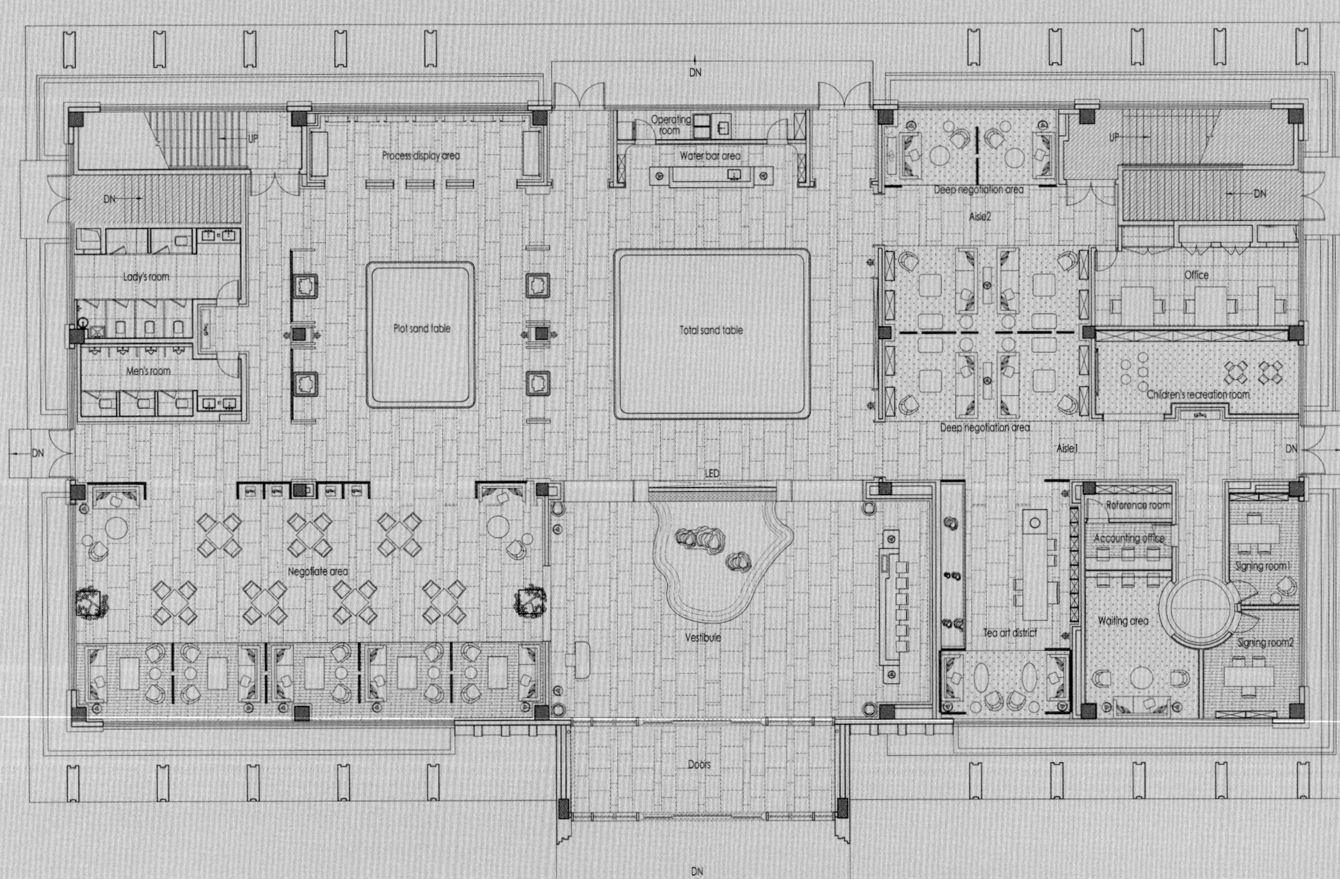

Floor plan

江山铭
坤达

Project:
Office Building of Hejia Home

Client:
Hejia Home

Location:
Jinan

The Art of Peace and Tranquil

As the poem of *Rice Transplanting* in the Tang Dynasty goes, when transplanting green seedlings all over the field, you greet the sky mirrored by water. Only a clean and peaceful mind can guide you, and stepping back brings you forward. The scene where people step backwards to transplant rice shoots illustrates the philosophy of life. "Hejia" stands for collaborate, implying a modest and peaceful lifestyle of entrepreneurs. The working elements like natural stone and wood infused into the austere design language create a clean and elegant working space.

Main materials: White Sand and Rice Yellow Marble, Straight Line White Jade Marble, Castle Rice Yellow Marble, Oak, and Walnut
Area: 1,500 m^2
Design time: July 2016
Completion time: August 2017

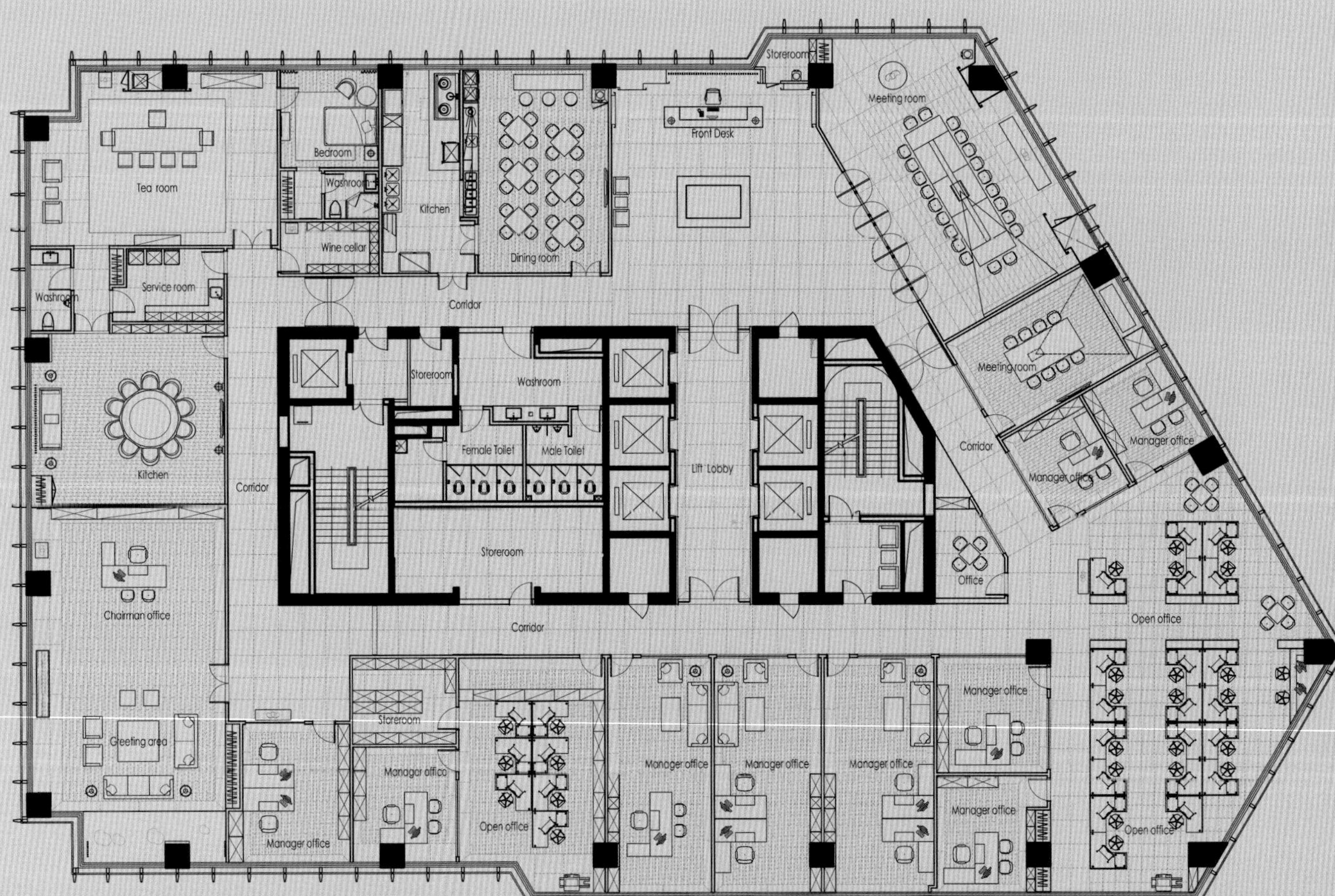

Floor plan

合|稼|置|业
HEJIAHOME

JINAN YEAR BOOK

Project:
Sales Center of Guangming Impression

Client:
Shengdijia Group

Location:
Puning

Moonrise by the Sea

"Spring sees river tide rise just as that in the sea, where the bright moon is rising along with the tide." Zhang Ruoxu, a poet of the Tang Dynasty, used the spring river, tide, sea and bright moon to depict a magnificent scene under the moon in all its grandeur and glory. It not only broadly brushes the joy of life but digs deep into the meaning of life as well. This project combines the essence of Chinese and western culture through pervaded allusion to the inherited construction practices of traditional Lingnan buildings. Not only does it find the commonality between the east and west but also boasts uniqueness, bringing the essence of "moon rising along with the tide" alive.

Main materials: Gold Mocca Marble, Purple Landscape Marble, and Blackwood
Area: 1,500 m^2
Design time: November 2017
Completion time: October 2018

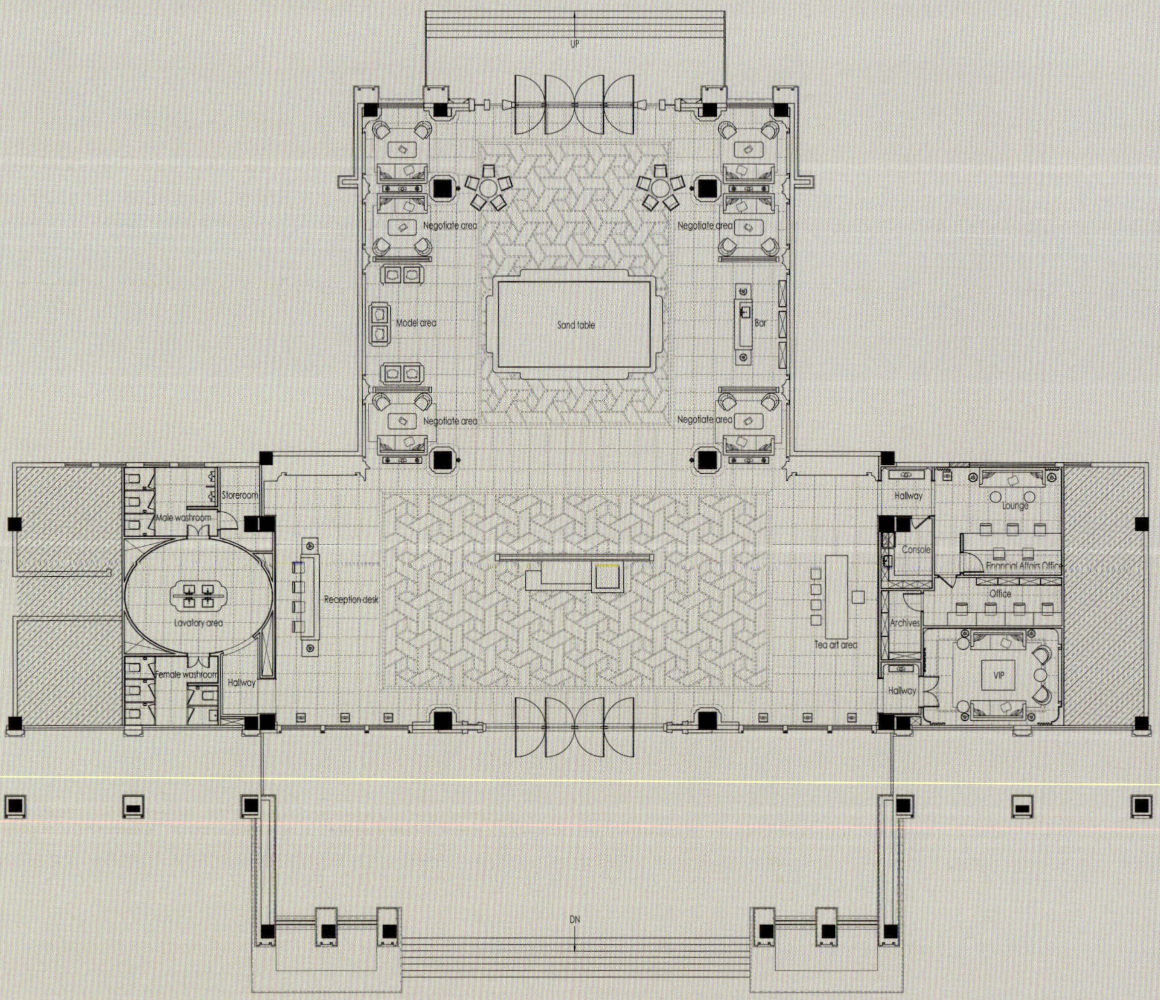

Floor plan

HONOUR IM

揭阳
河源
揭西
广州
大南山
惠州
深汕合作区
珠三角
深圳
惠来

Project:
Show House of International Plaza

Client:
Wanhao Real Estate

Location:
Yichang

Ripples in the Sunshine and Mountain Afar

This project creates a space of Chinese style with modern simplicity. The throwback to the aesthetics of the Song Dynasty revitalizes an artistic life of leisure and comfort. "Warblers chirp on willows in spring times. A curl of mist sees ripples in the sunshine and mountain afar." Those sceneries perfectly echo with landscape outside window, and consist of a beautiful scroll of ink painting. Designers connect nature and living space in a creative manner, and give space a touch of quietness, which originates from nature but goes beyond nature.

Main materials: Ink South Marble, Silver Silk Marble, Brown Marble, Walnut and Silk Cloth
Area: 260 m^2
Design time: March 2017
Completion time: December 2017

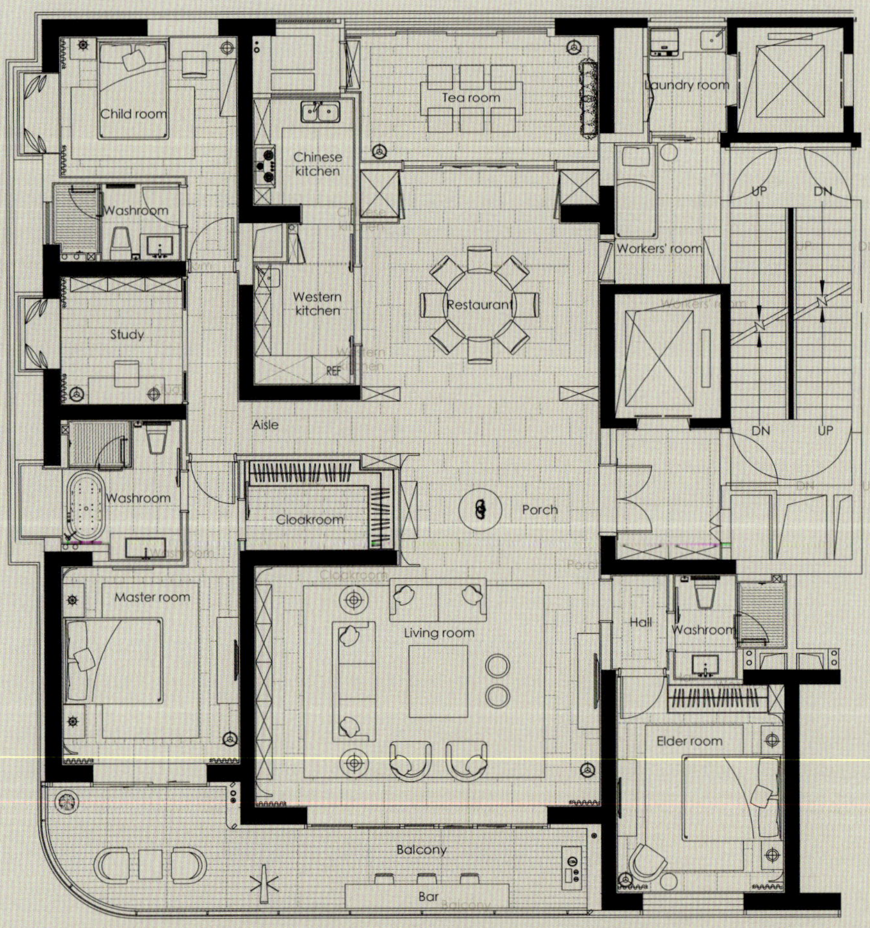

Floor plan

Neo-Chinese Elegance
优雅新中式

Project:
Guangming No.1 Show House

Client:
Shengdijia Group

Location:
Puning

Visiting Garden

As Mr. Tong Jun said in the Annals of Gardens in the South of the Yangtze River, the design and arrangements of gardens shall not rigidly played by the book and limited by rules, but should be full of characters and vibrancy. The focus of garden design lies in improvisation, while pleasure and diversity should be the priority of visiting a garden. Against the modern background, designers integrate modern mindset with oriental aesthetics, and provide "visitors" with a good visiting experience. The seemingly "simple and clean" design implicitly carries a unique understanding and thinking of Chinese aesthetics, full of freehand brushwork with subtlety of meticulous techniques.

Main materials: Silver Gray Stone, Versailles Gold Marble, Walnut, Wallpaper, Cloth
Area: 240 m^2
Design time: April 2017
Completion time: May 2018

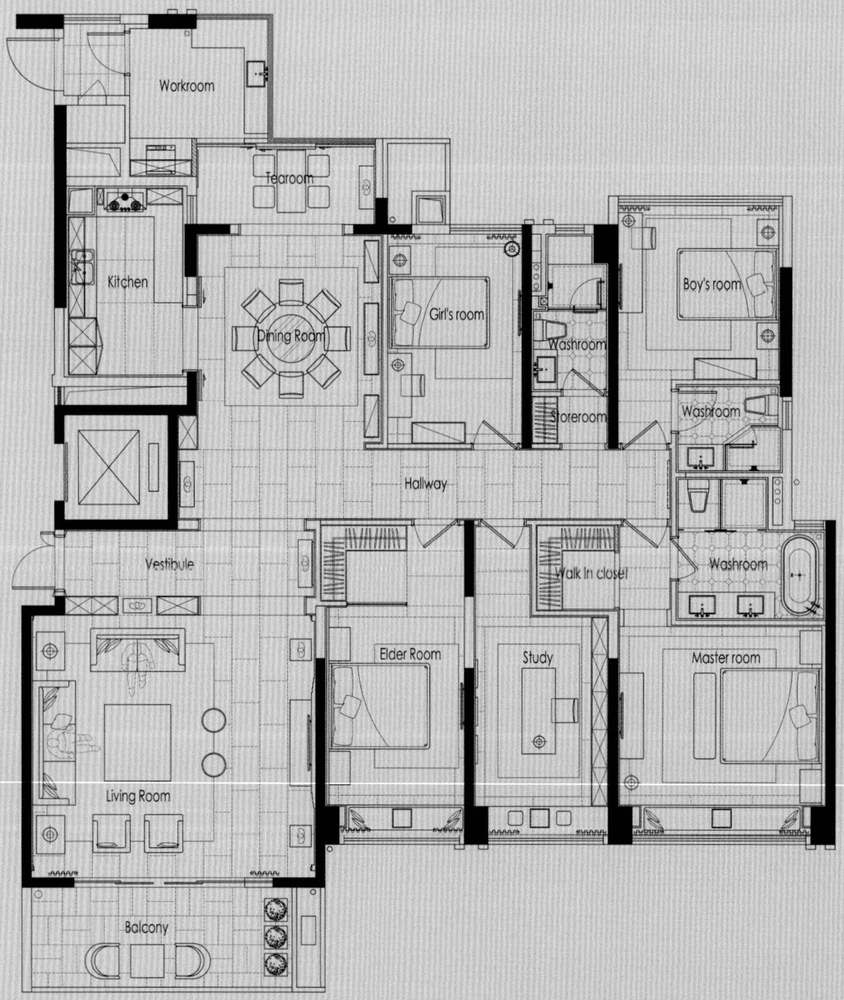

Floor plan

Project:
Beihu No.1 Chamber

Client:
Anar Group

Location:
Beijing

Among Rivers and Mountains

When designers probe into the core of design and pursue diversity, inspirations ensue with their deeper understanding of humanity and nature. The essence of mountain and water space lies in the word "space". When strolling in nature sceneries, you unexpectedly find different views in every step. "Space" bridges nature and human beings. This design combines the Eastern space aesthetics with western artistic taste, and finds its footing in classical elements when constructing a diversified space with distinctly modern art flair, where restraint and boldness collide in a timeless way.

Main materials: New Cloud Grey Marble, Ink Jade Marble, Purple Landscape Marble, Walnut, Wallpaper, and Cloth
Area: 860 m^2
Design time: March 2017
Completion time: February 2018

Plan of the first floor

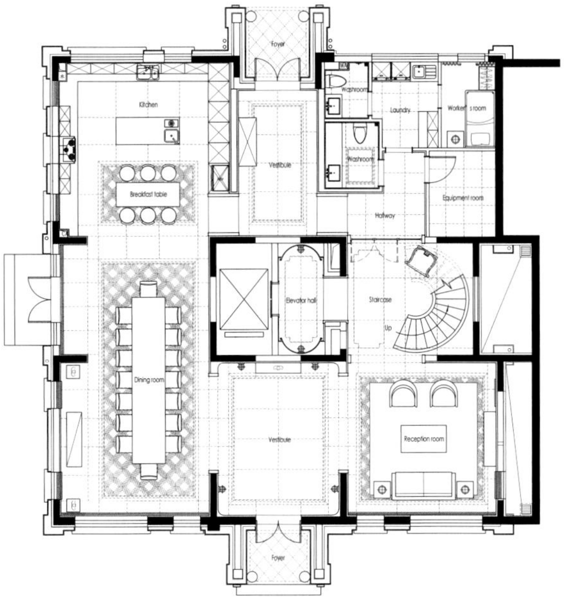

Plan of the basement

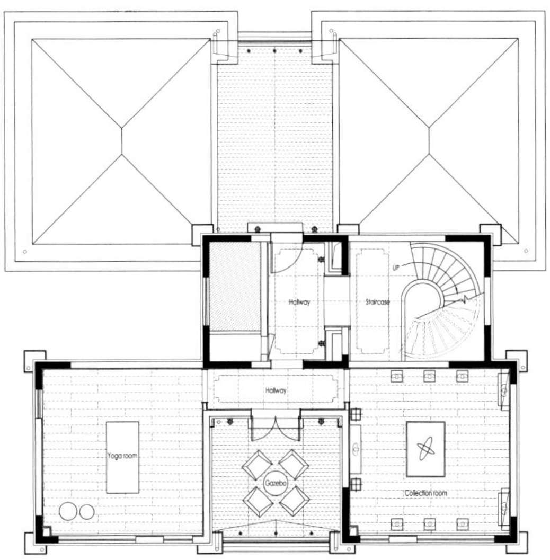

Plan of the mezzanine floor

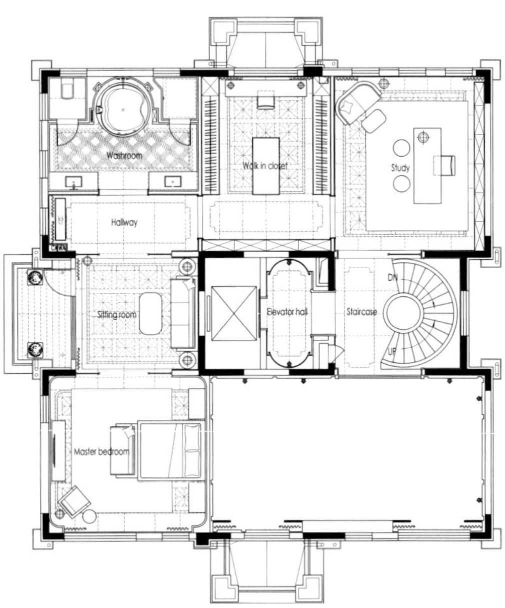

Plan of the second floor

Project:
Beverly Estate Villa

Client:
Central China Real Estate

Location:
Xinxiang

Expressing Feelings

Space aesthetics refer to life aesthetics. The literati in the Song Dynasty have refined elegance and pure beauty of life in their daily life, a supreme state of "slow living" that attracts modern people most. This project takes refined aesthetics of Eastern simplicity as the core of design, providing experience of elegant Eastern space and expressing the pursuit of humanity aesthetics. You can feel quality and meaning given to life through each displayed detail.

Main materials: Prague Grey Marble, Landscape Pattern Marble, Walnut, Oak, Wallpaper and Cloth
Area: 280 m^2
Design time: January 2017
Completion time: September 2017

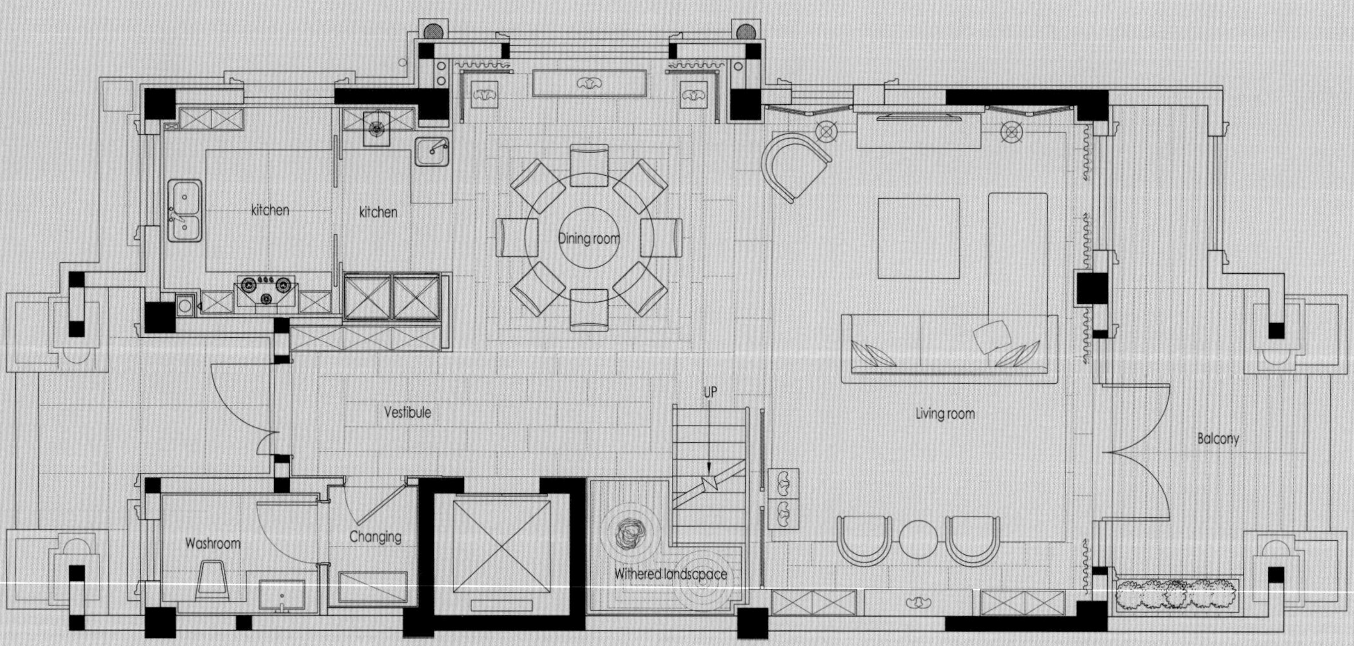

Plan of the first floor

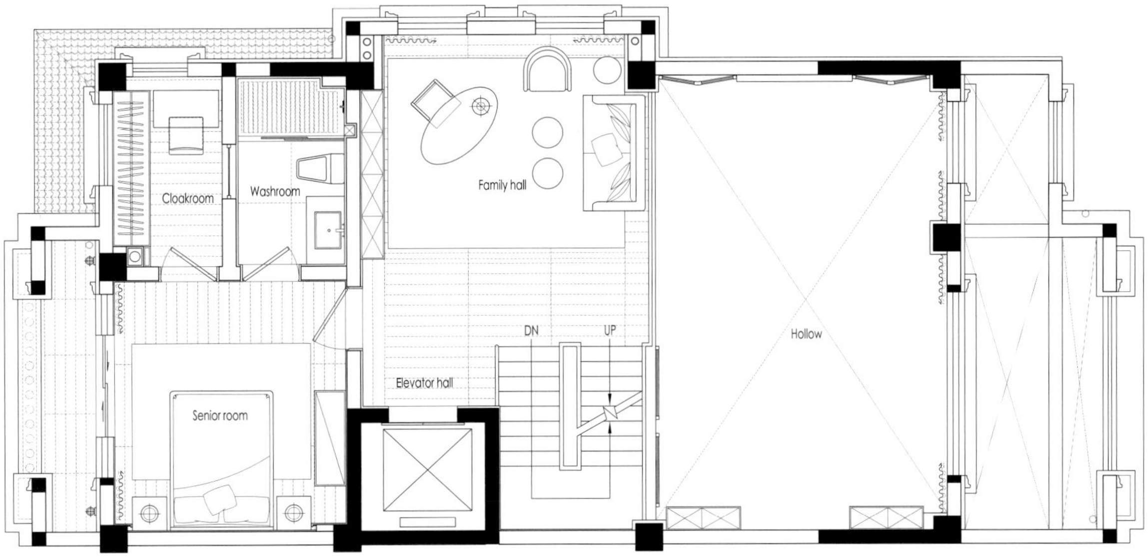

Plan of the second floor

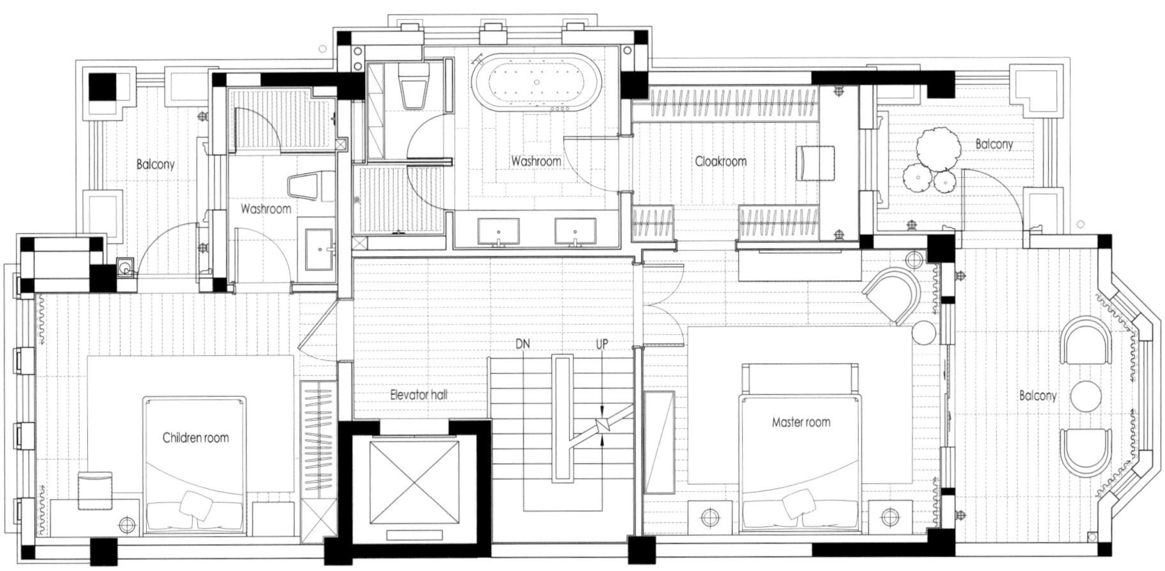

Plan of the third floor

Project:
Show House of Longhu Bay

Client:
Faithland Group

Location:
Jiangmen

Cloud from the East

As written in *Jiuge Dongjun* by Qu Yuan, "Wearing beautiful clothes like clouds, he raised his bow and shot at the constellation Sirius." According to China's "five elements" theory, the east belongs to wood and its color is green, and therefore "green cloud" also equals to the east cloud. In this project, designers create an archaic atmosphere on the basis of oriental elements. It showcases modern exploration in Chinese culture, and brings a brand-new visual experience through tracing back to traditional Chinese patterns, colors and elements. In doing so, the paintings of contemporary artist incorporated with fineness shine through.

Main materials: Silver Gray Marble, Bronze Stainless Steel, Oak, Walnut and Latex Paint
Area: 160 m^2
Design time: January 2016
Completion time: July 2016

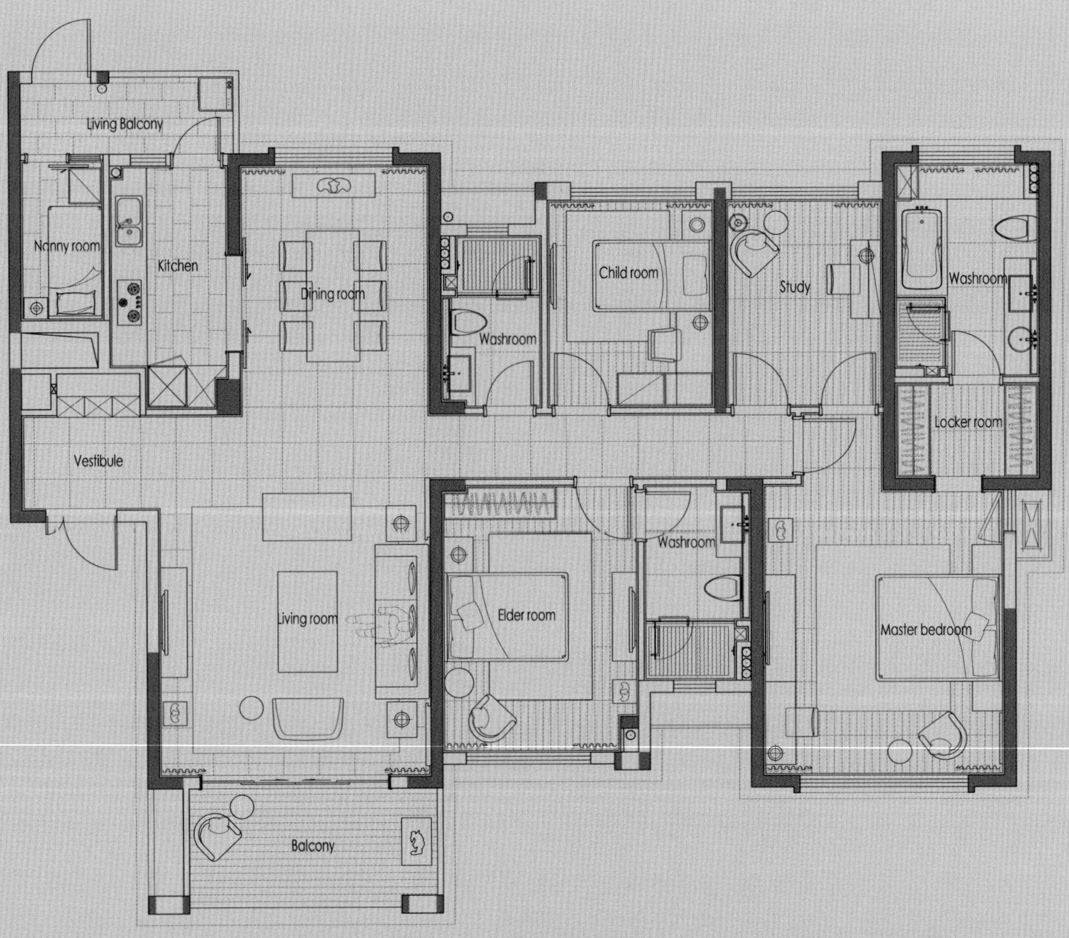

Floor Plan

Project:
Show House of Tianjunhui

Client:
RK Properties

Location:
Foshan

Brightness

This project borrows the concept of Lingnan's famous garden name "Brightness" to create a bright, clean and graceful space. This elegant and beautiful design embodies the simplicity of contemporary art of the east through restrained elaboration. By using unique local culture symbols to express the elegance of Lingnan culture, it delivers a refined experience in harmony with the Lingnan customs to the dweller.

Main materials: White Gold Sand Marble, Landscape Pattern Marble, Oak, Hand-Painted Wallpaper and Bronze Stainless Steel
Area: 354 m^2
Design time: May 2018
Completion time: May 2019

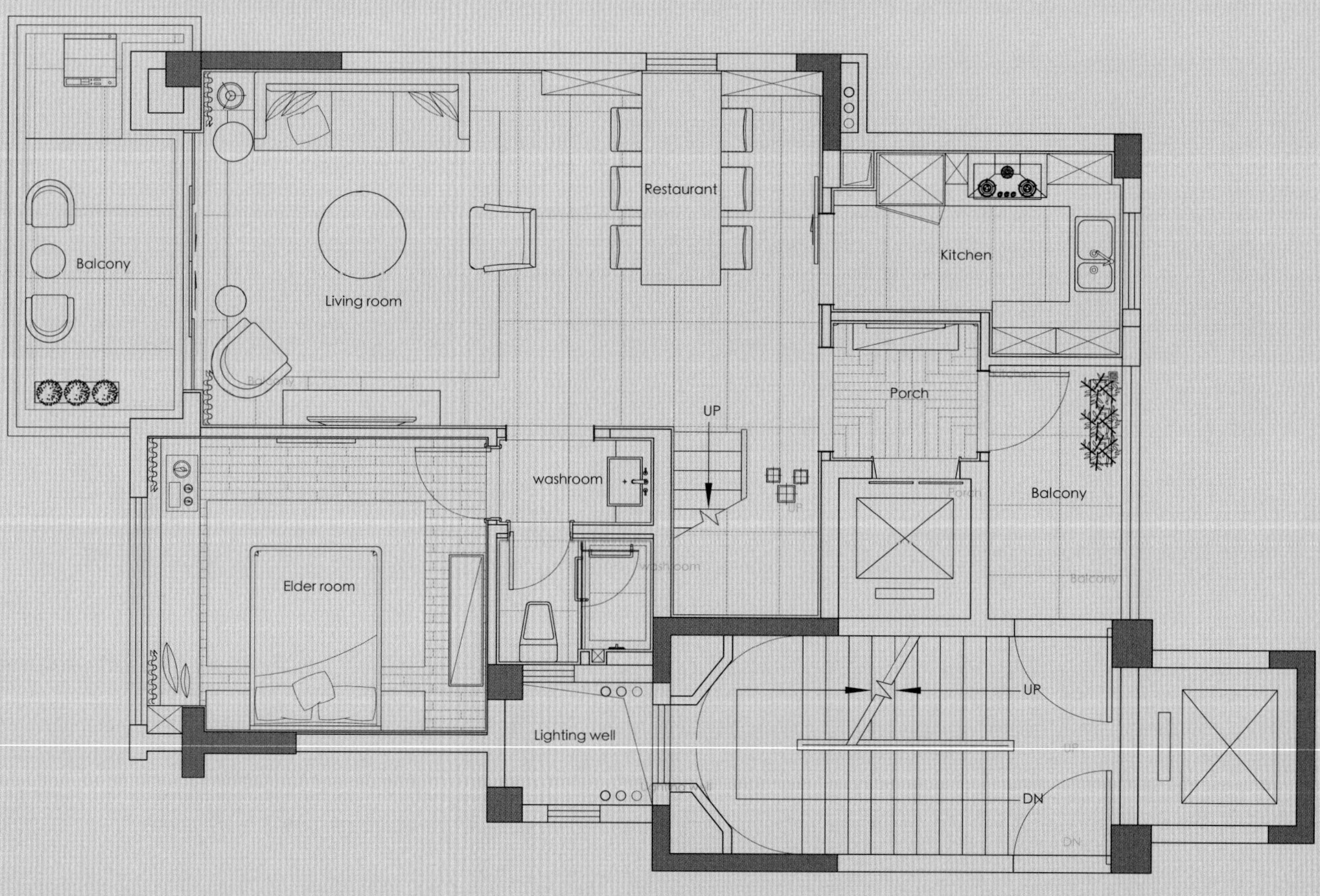

Plan of the third floor

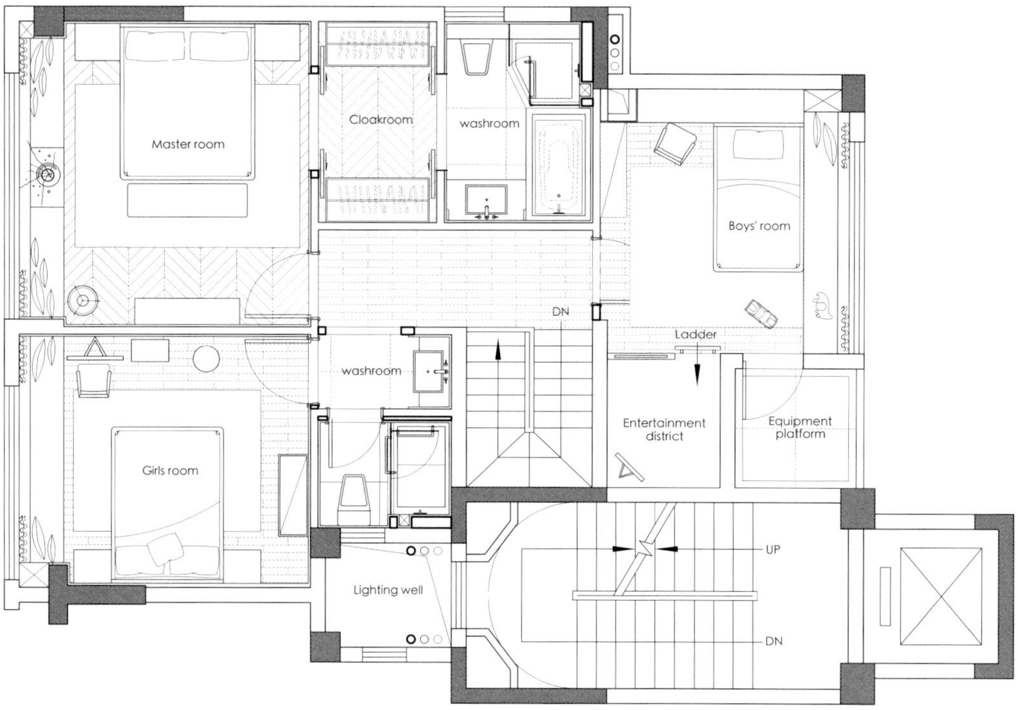

Plan of the fourth floor

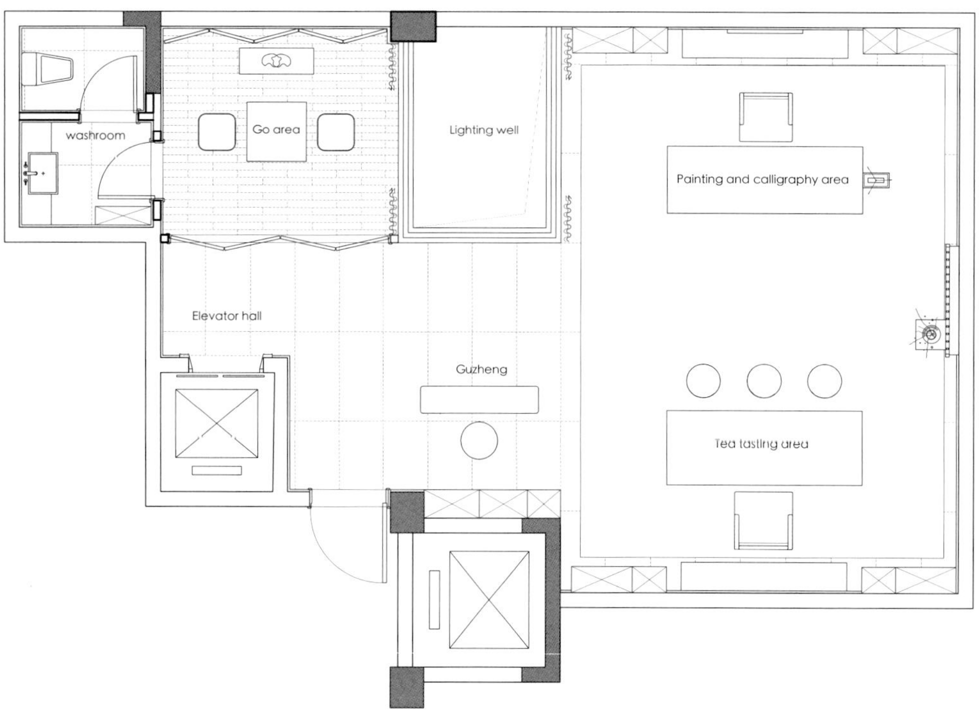

Plan of the mezzaine floor

Project:
Show House of Caifu Chamber

Client:
Caifu Zhiye

Location:
Nanyang

Learning from Ancient Times

This project integrates modern thinking with Eastern aesthetics, brimming with the vivacious spirit of bold brushwork with meticulous techniques. In this mansion full of thoughtfulness and culture, every detail gives you the realness of a modern space with Chinese style.

Main materials: Ness High Grey Marble, Wood Pattern Marble, Oak, Hand-Painted Wallpaper and Art Glass
Area: 278 m^2
Design time: November 2018
Completion time: April 2019

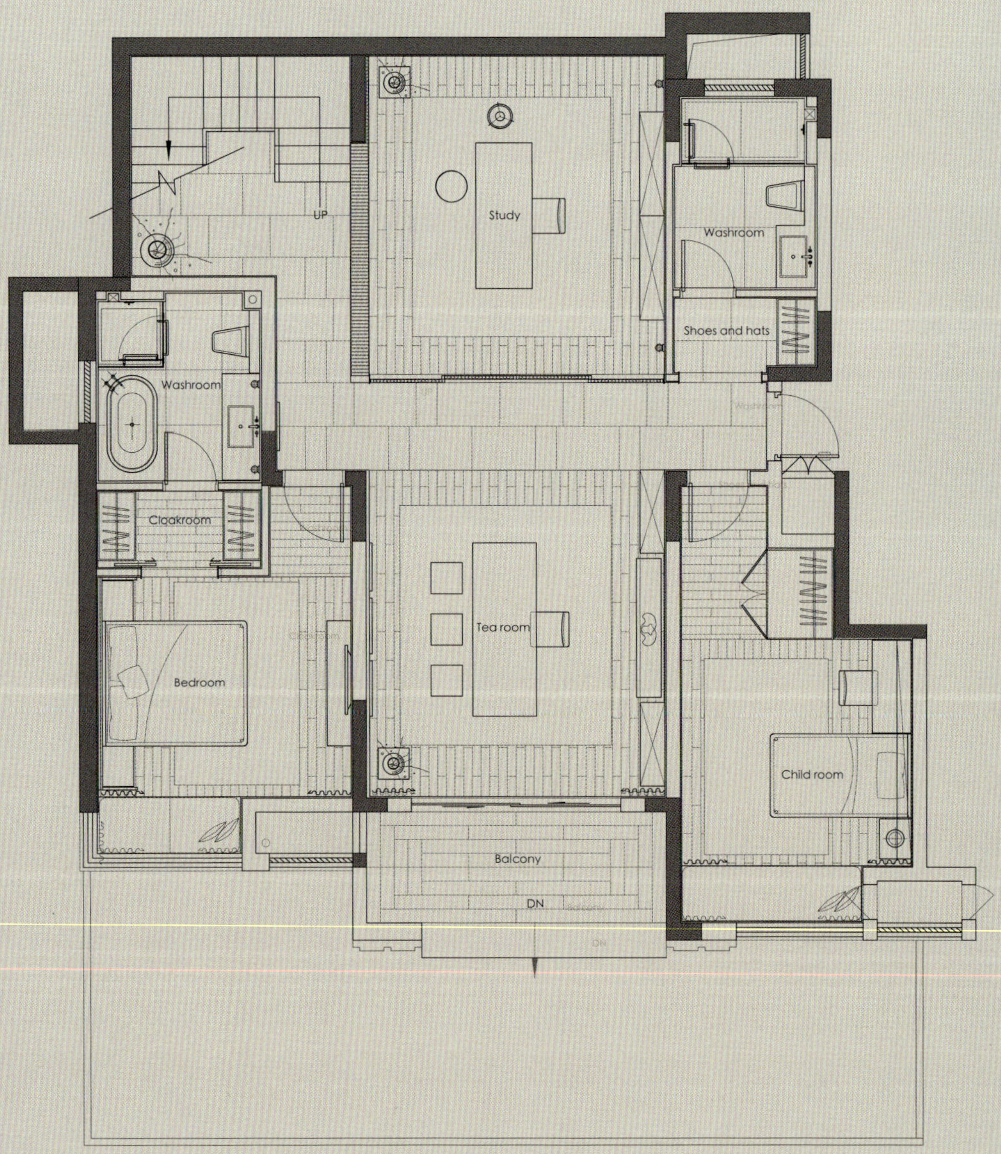

Plan of the first floor

Neo-Chinese Elegance

Plan of the second floor

Project:
Show House of Tianjunhui

Client:
RK Properties

Location:
Foshan

Comfort and Elegance

Comfort and elegance refer to the respect of beauty. It shows the charm of Chinese language and culture heritages. Elegancy and nobleness exude from these characters. The aesthetic style of this project is luxurious outside, elegance inside, offering a unique and unconventional residence for urban elites with style and attitude.

Main materials: Snow Flake Marble, Brazilian Tile Gray Marble, Flamed Maple, Oak, and Black Stainless Steel
Area: 275 m^2
Design time: May 2018
Completion time: May 2019

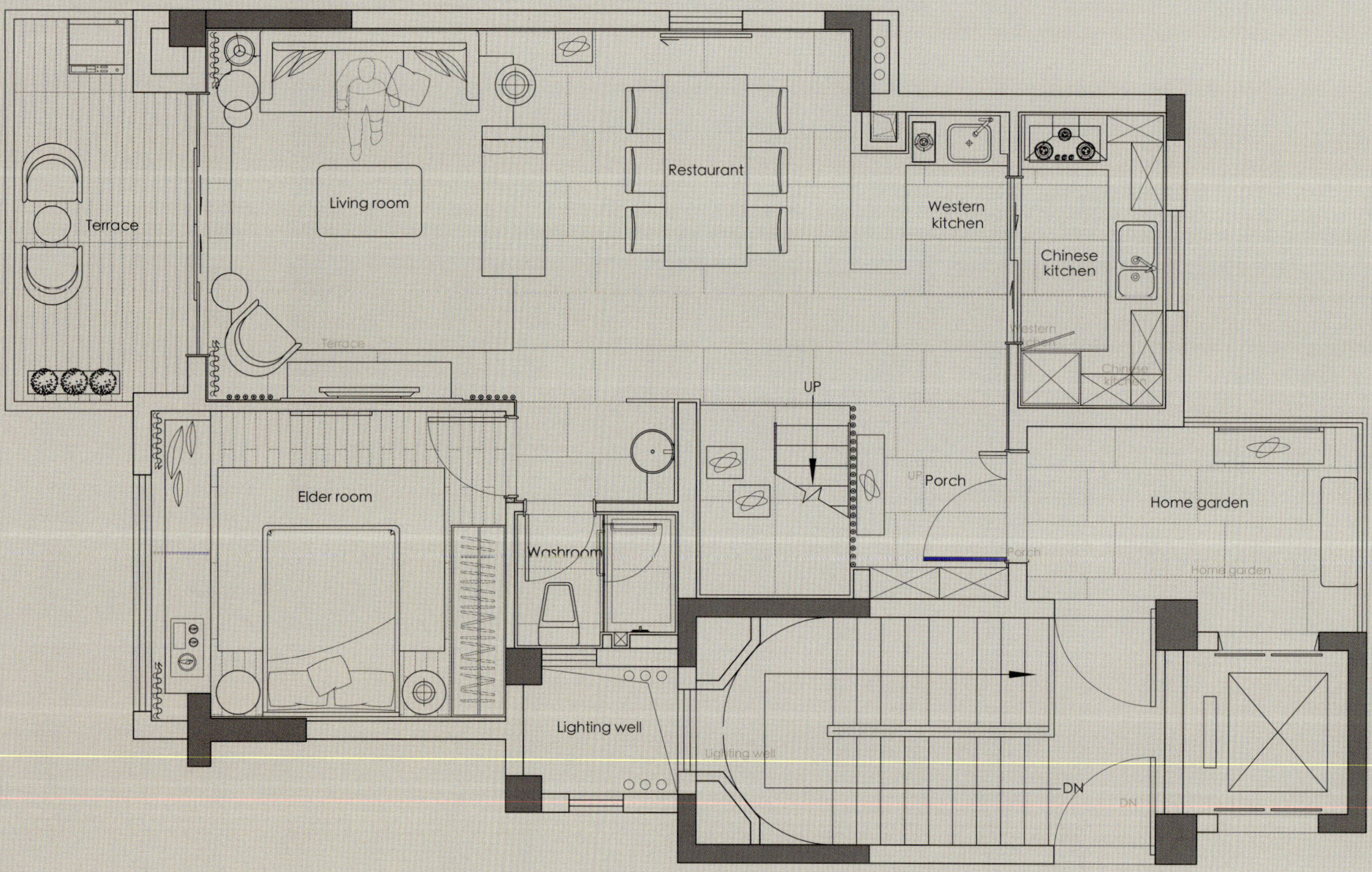

Plan of the fifth floor

Naoto Fukasawa
EMBODIMENT

Plan of the sixth floor

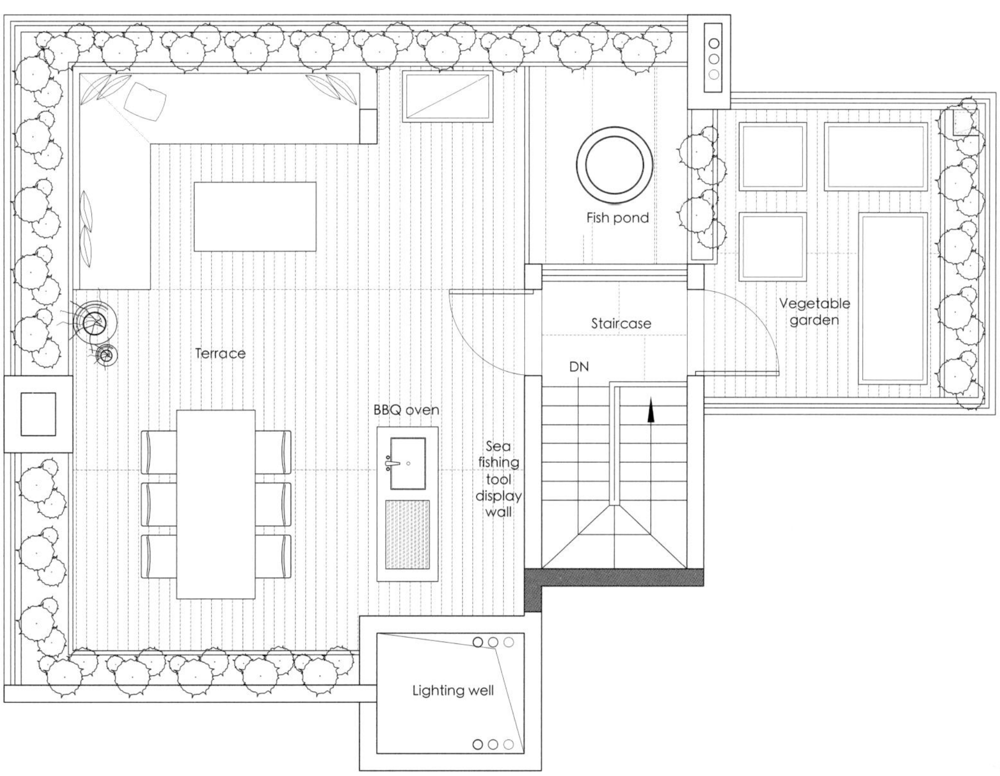

Plan of the seventh floor

FOLIO-02
CLOTHING
The art of libraries
WYETH
spring trend BOOK
AC DC
FOR THOSE ABOUT TO
ROCK

A brief history of the

Project:
Show House of Swan Lake

Client:
OTC Properties

Location:
Foshan

Mountains in the Mist

"Amid the mist, countless green mountains stand in the distance. The afterglow of the sunset touches the back of the flying wild geese where tinges of red fade away." As written by Zhou Bangyan, a poet in the Song Dynasty, in *Yulouchun* - Taoxi Stream Refuses to Stay, the mist, mountains, wild geese, sunset, and glow of the sun create a poetic sunset landscape. Here you can find that poetic, humanistic and natural elements become a harmonious blend, which polishes modern styles that are held dear in metropolis. The temperate earth tones give away calm and warm feelings, echoing the scenery of lakes and mountains outside.

Main materials: White Sand Rice Yellow Marble, Peacock Blue Jade, Gold Jade Marble, Walnut, Bronze Stainless Steel and Wallpaper
Area: 250 m^2
Design time: March 2016
Completion time: December 2016

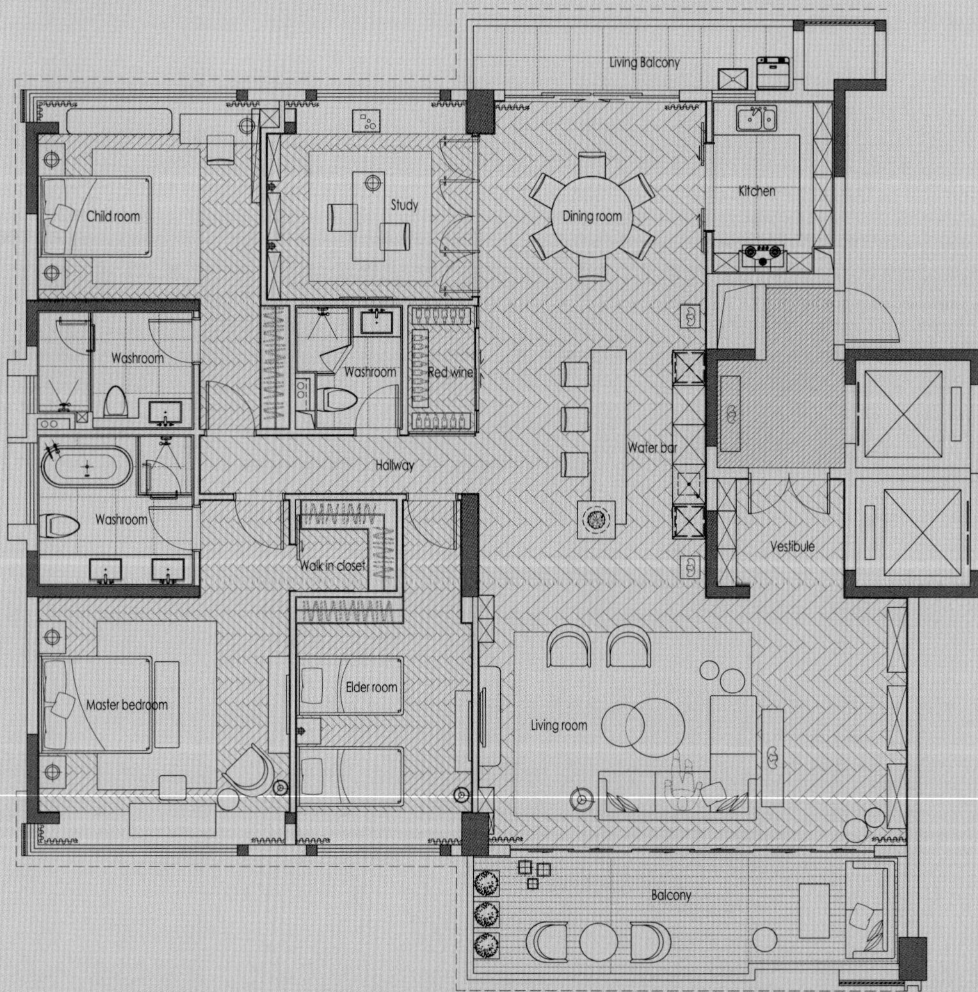

Floor plan

Project:
Show House of Guoshanshu

Client:
Zhongqi Properties

Location:
Taian

Viewing the Mountain

Guoshanshu, against Mount Tai, the head of the five mountains, perfectly combines the enjoyment of living besides Mount Tai to the convenience that comes with a city center. Looking at the mountain has been a unique joy for the Chinese people since ancient times, as well as a source of inspiration for many scholars and writers. In this project, the noble atmosphere permeates every corner of the room. Art furnishings are used to enhance cultural experience. Mountain, nature and Chinese elements finally come together naturally in this work.

Main materials: Slawomir Peszko Gray Marble, Wood Pattern Marble, New Sand Rice Yellow Marble, Sea Pattern Jade Marble, Walnut, and Bronze Stainless Steel
Area: 800 m^2
Design time: March 2016
Completion time: October 2016

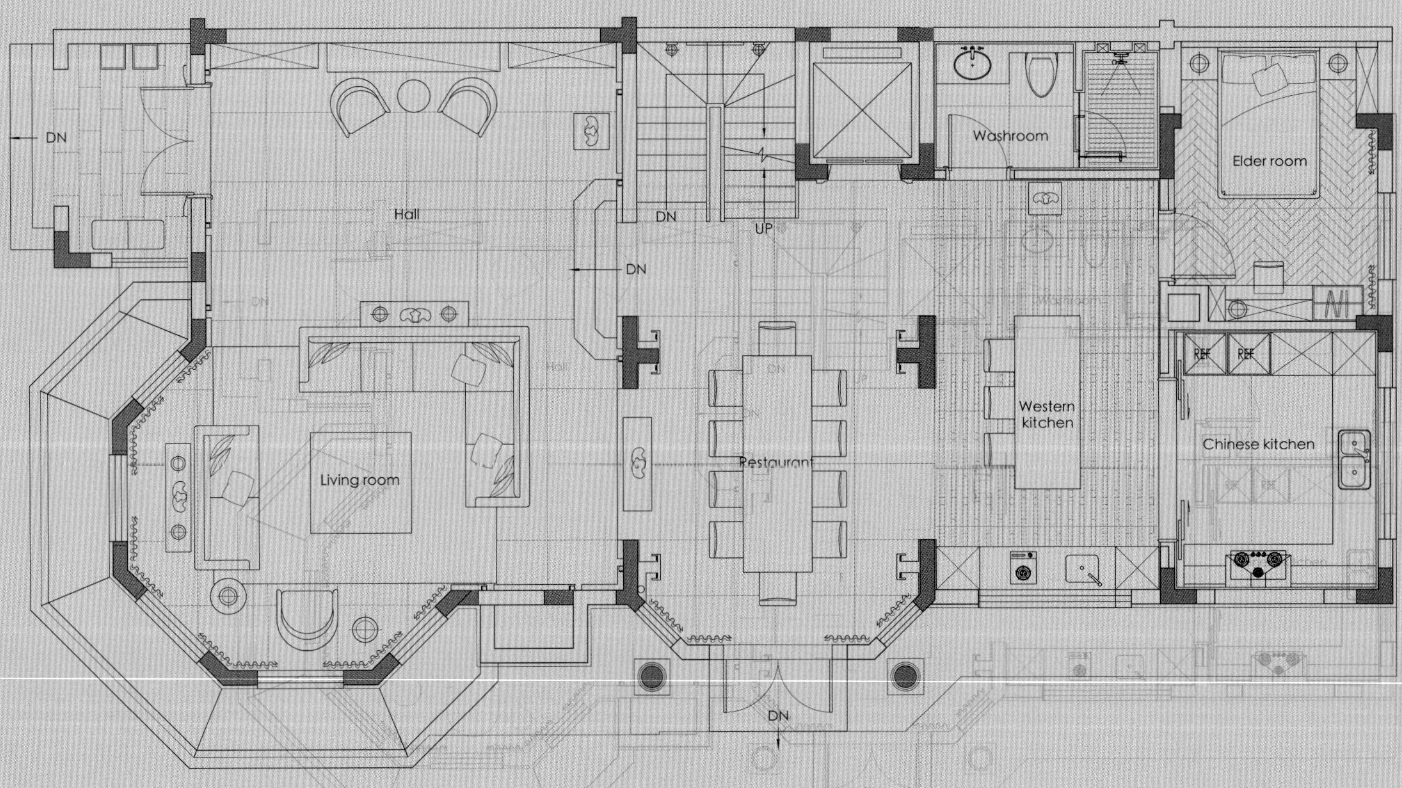

Plan of the first floor

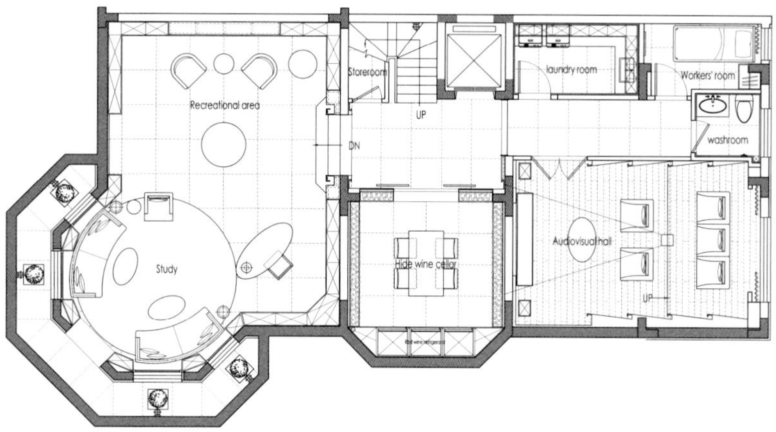

Plan of the basement

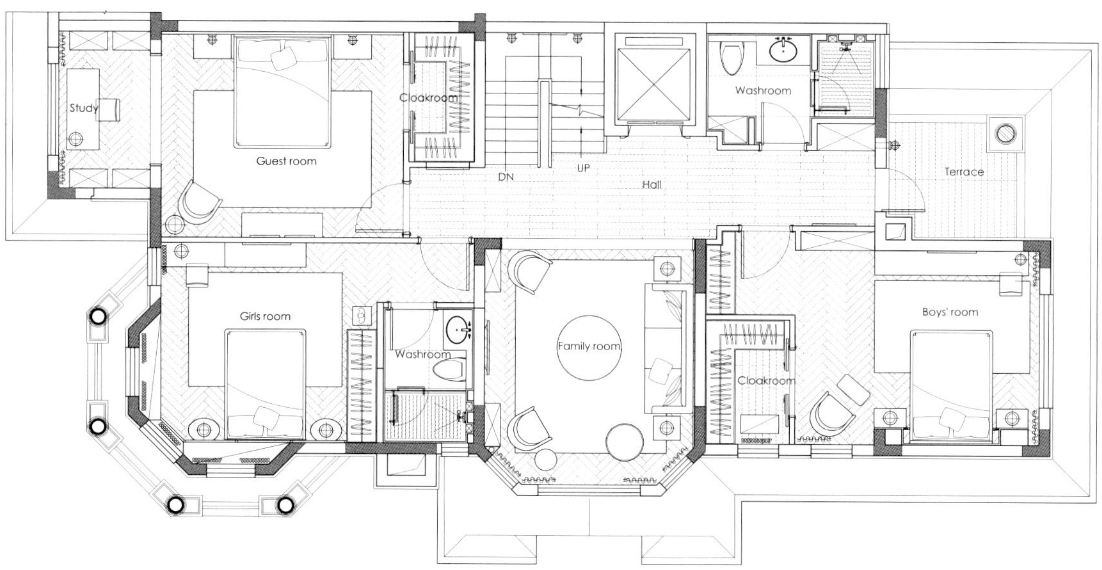

Plan of the second floor

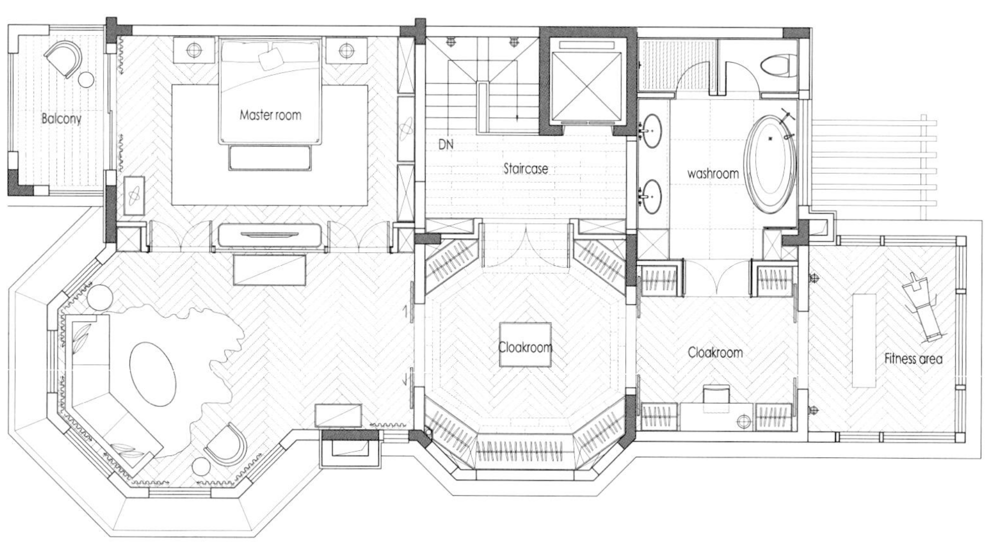

Plan of the third floor

Project:
Show House of Guoshanshu

Client:
Zhongqi Properties

Location:
Taian

Toasting and Cheering

"Wine glasses mingle with each other and friends sit up and down from time to time. This is the joy of the guests." What a joy of living in mountains and waters. In this project, the spacious indoor penetrated by elegant arcs, emerges a smooth moving line, or a seemingly nonexistent boundary. As the main tone, earthy color embellishes the room with warmth and gives an elegant vibe for guests entertain here.

Main materials: Snow Flake White Marble, Snow Mountain Lotus Marble, Flamed Maple, Leather and Hand-Painted Wallpaper
Area: 253 m^2
Design time: December 2017
Completion time: August 2018

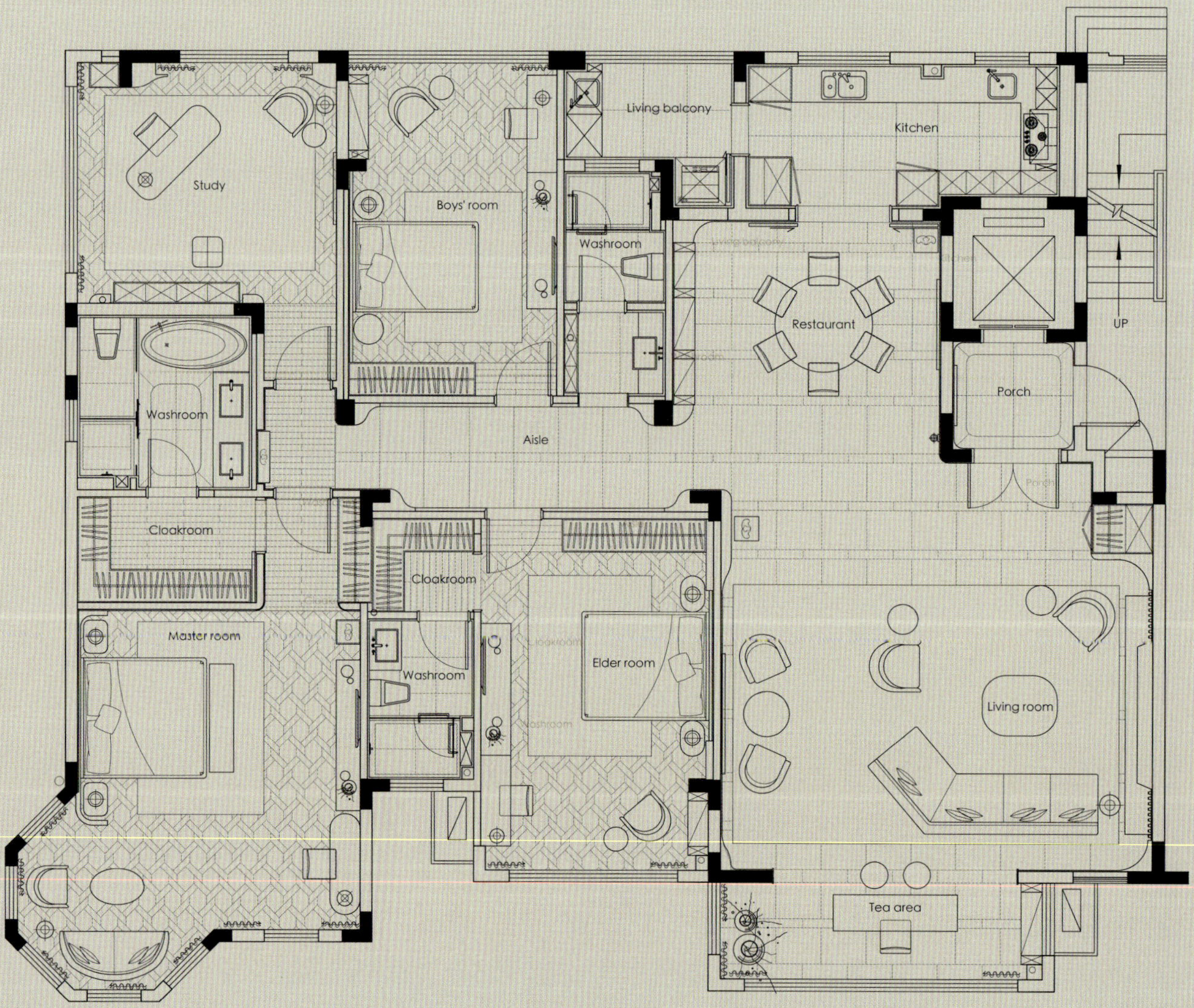

Floor plan

REMARKABLE HERITAGE HOUSES
Mother and Child

Project:
Soft Furnishings for Show House of Jiangwancheng

Client:
Haishu Chengtou Real Estate

Location:
Ningbo

Blossom in the Spring

Beautiful flowers bloom in the spring, accompanied by the charming songs from the birds. A wonderful picture coming up with pleasing sound and vision. Soft furnishings are designed based on the regional aesthetic appeal. Visual presentation is determined with elegance and fashion as the standard as an endeavor to create a strong sense of place and bring residents the experience of a deluxe living style.

Area: 240 m^2
Design time: August 2016
Completion time: January 2017

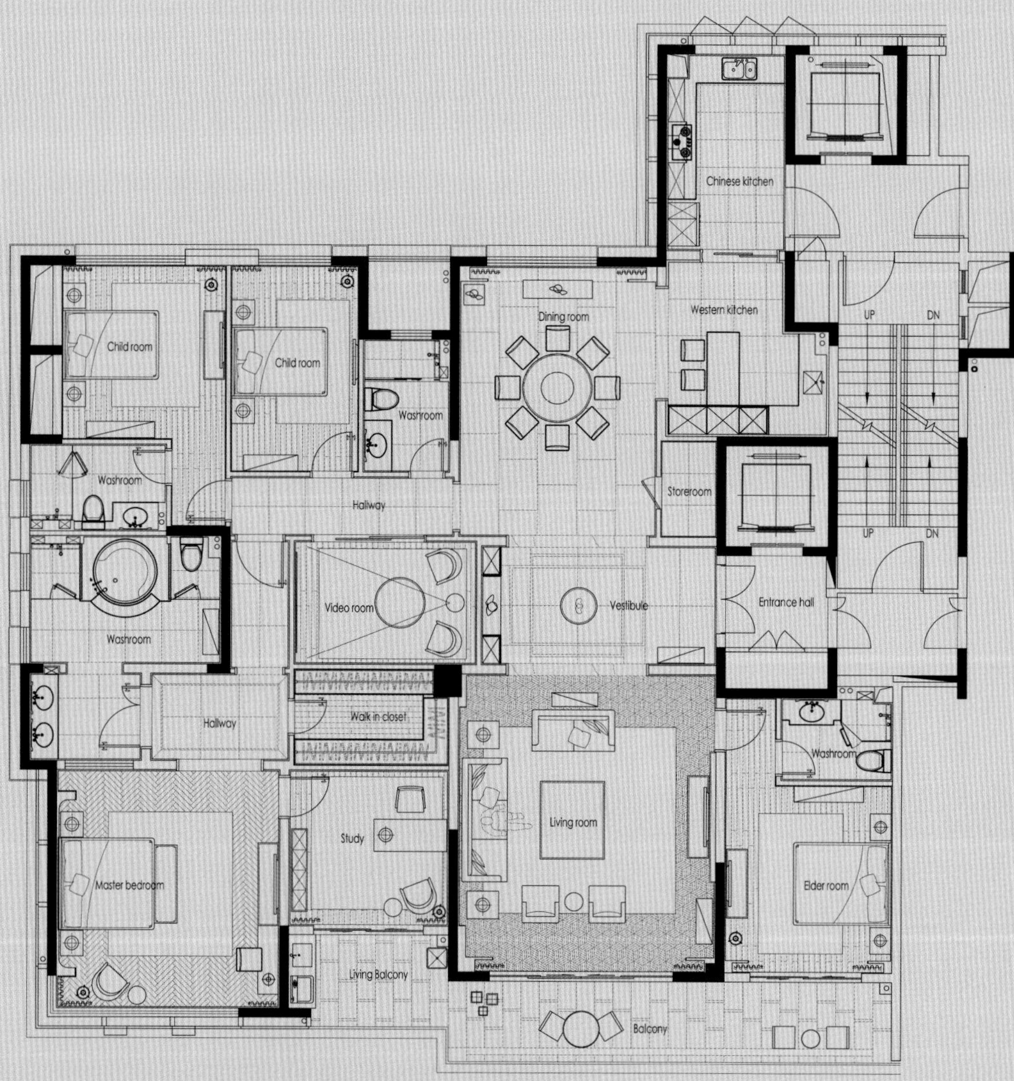

Floor plan

Make It Fabulous

ZAO WOU-KI
ŒUVRES 1935-2008
Flammarion

WKW
THE CINEMA OF WONG KAR WAI
Make It Fabulous
The Architecture & Designs of William T. Georgis
ROOMS FOR LIVING

Project:
Soft Furnishings for Show House of Jiangwancheng

Client:
Haishu Chengtou Real Estate

Location:
Ningbo

A Soft Blanket of Pure White

The space wrapped in a soft blanket of pure white is beautiful and stately. The interplay between light and shadow captures the enchanting beauty, presenting a picturesque and refreshing view. The soft furnishings push the boundaries of style, deconstruct popular culture, and re-examine the art of furnishings and life through the lens of humanity.

Area: 240 m^2
Design time: September 2017
Completion time: June 2018

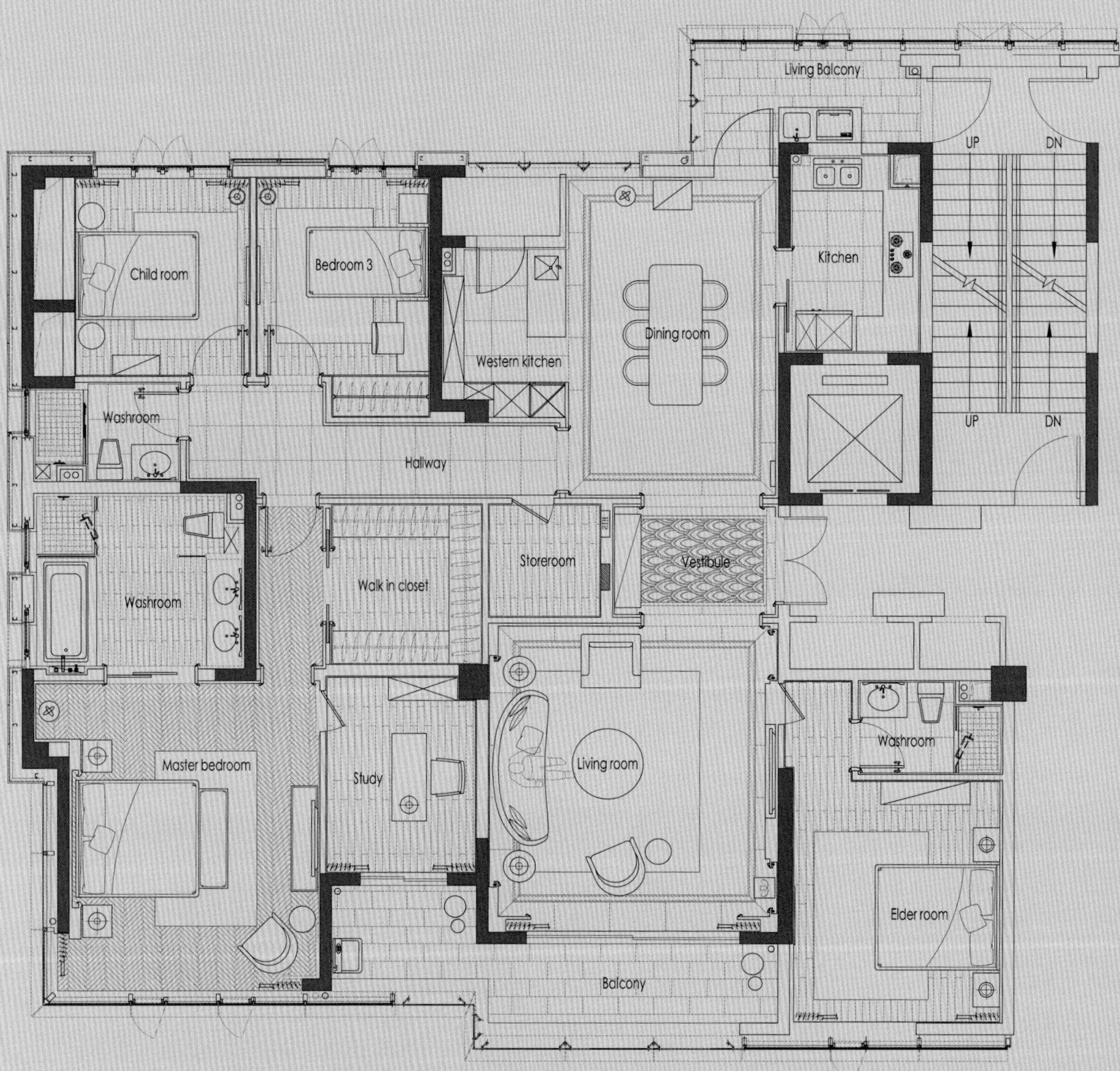

Floor plan

DALÍ
FASHION
Impressionist Art
MONET
TASCHEN
BARABAIG
Charles Lane
CHAUMET

Project:
Show House of International Plaza

Client:
Wanhao Real Estate

Location:
Yichang

Enjoyable Life by a Mist-covered River

The property stands by a river in Yichang, the territory of the ancient State of Chu, offering a view of the green mountains and mist-covered river. In tribute to the landscape, this design expresses a yearning for an enjoyable life. It interprets the ideal of luxurious life, and sets the trend of fashion design.

Main materials: Blue Gold Sand, Cold Jade Marble, Oak, Bronze Stainless Steel, and Art Glass
Area: 210 m^2
Design time: March 2017
Completion time: December 2017

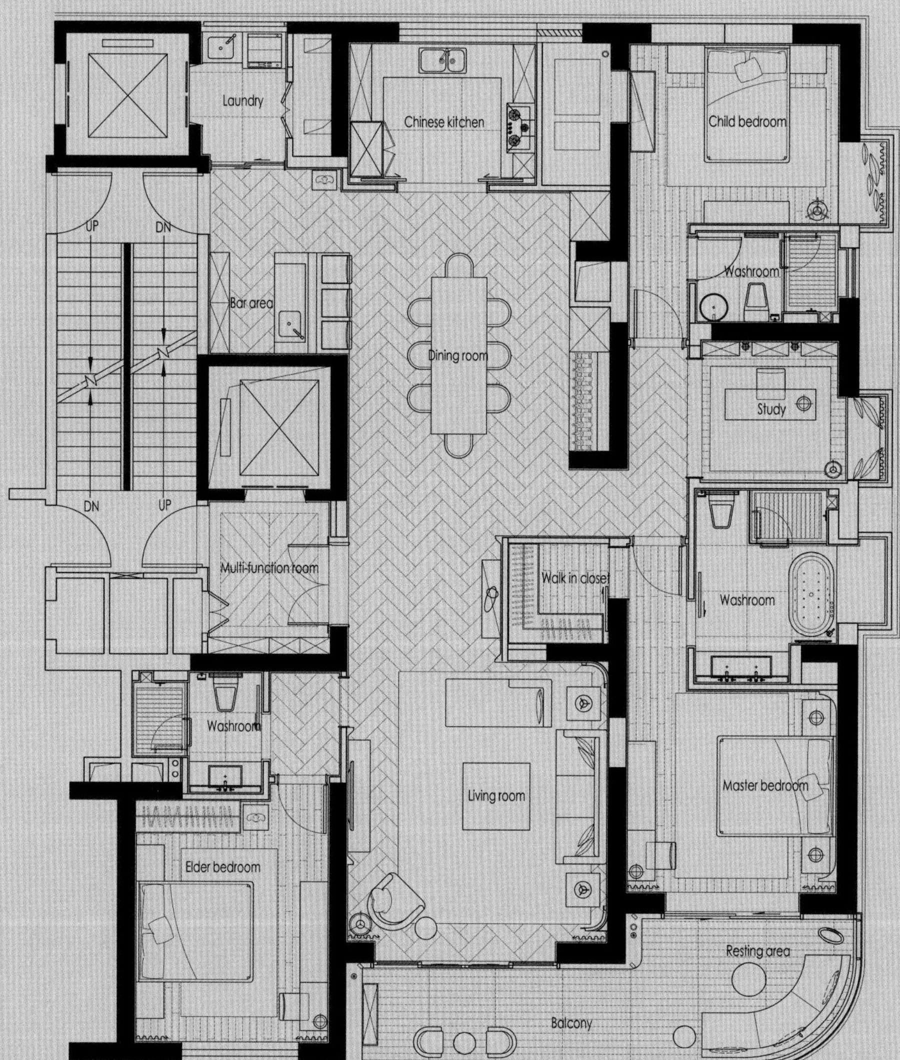

Floor plan

Project:
Sales Center of Bright Stars

Client:
Faithland Group

Location:
Dongguan

A Poetic Touch

The design extends the expression of natural aesthetics from a modern perspective for a balance between poetry and life. The natural leaf-shaped chandelier echoes the scenery of the park nearby. The geometric cutout design wall makes the space airier. Inspired by the beauty of all things on earth, the space is adorned by elements of nature. The interplay between light and shadow exudes the quiet and boundless sense of freedom. A dialogue that goes into our soul begins.

Main materials: Paris Grey Marble, Jazz White Marble, Oak, Bronze Stainless Steel, and Art Glass
Area: 700 m^2
Design time: August 2018
Completion time: March 2019

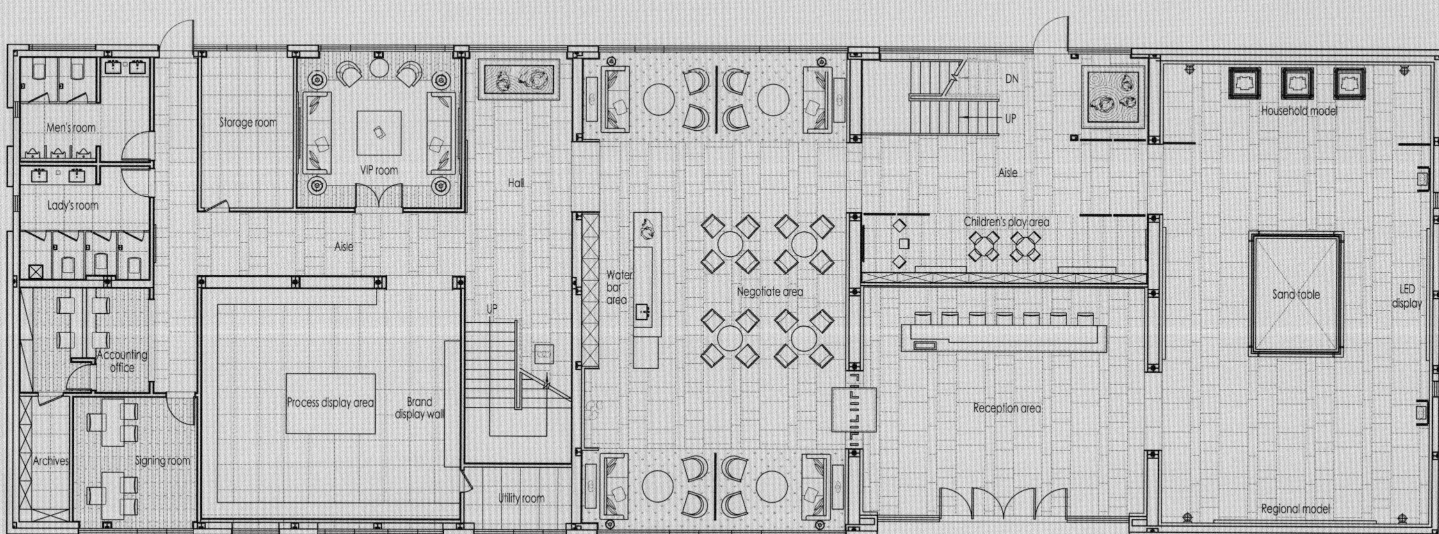

Floor plan

MARTELL
XO

Project:
Sales Center of Caihongli

Client:
Faithland Group

Location:
Huizhou

Rainbow

This is a cozy community built upon the concept of "neighborhood and sharing". Sunlight and water drops serve as a proper start of the interpretation of "rainbow", which is reinforced by decorative arts and bright contrasting colors. In this space, colors and shapes are used to evoke people's feelings while being part of the decoration. The arc ceiling echoes the theme "rainbow", dotted with lights to fill the space with vitality and warmth.

Main materials: Roman Grey Marble, Jazz White Marble, Oak, Bronze Stainless Steel, and Art Glass
Area: 1,600 m^2
Design time: November 2018
Completion time: May 2019

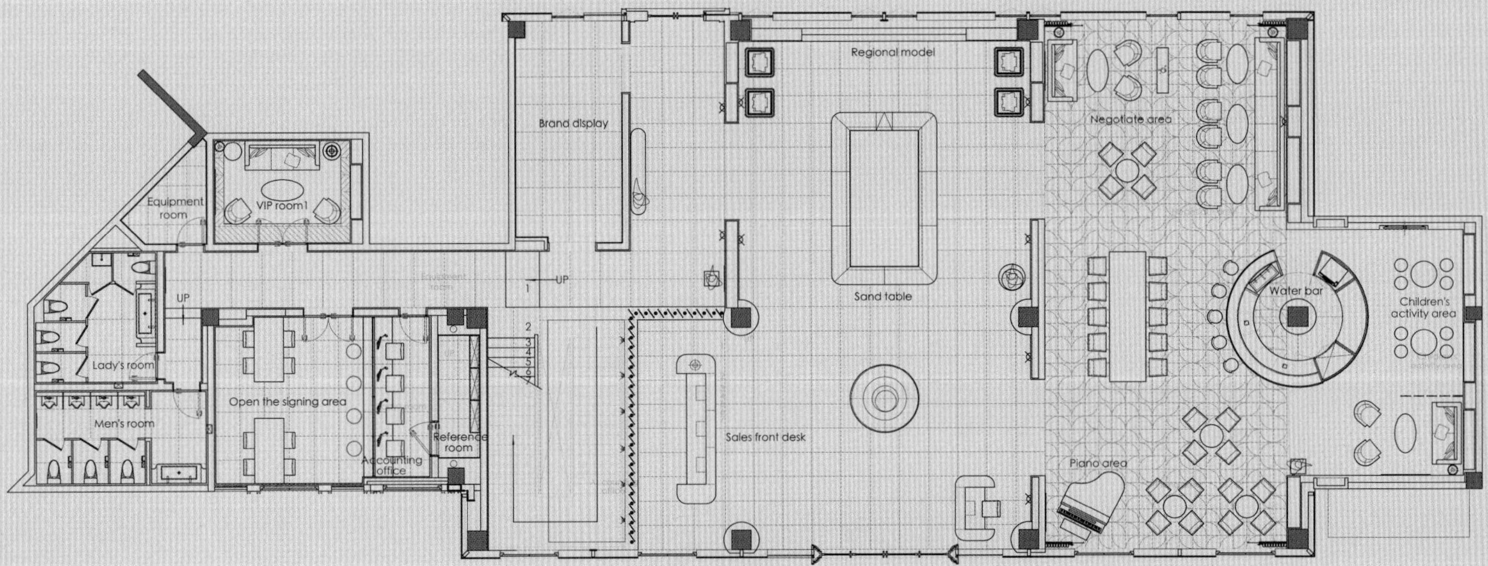

Floor plan

LOOKBOOK

Project:
Sales Center of Rainbow Residence

Client:
Faithland Group

Location:
Zhongshan

Crafting

Inspired by "sparking stars", the space brings together a fashionable and exquisite lifestyle and an artistic forest community. On the theme "artistic forest", modern and simple techniques are applied to express the poetic beauty through natural elements. A balance is struck among points, lines, surfaces, and blocks for simplicity, giving rise to a harmony of modern space between the natural and the artificial.

Main materials: Golden Jade Marble, Snow Mountain Flying Fox Marble, Snowflake White Marble, Art Paint, and Art Glass
Area: 840 m^2
Design time: July 2019
Completion time: November 2019

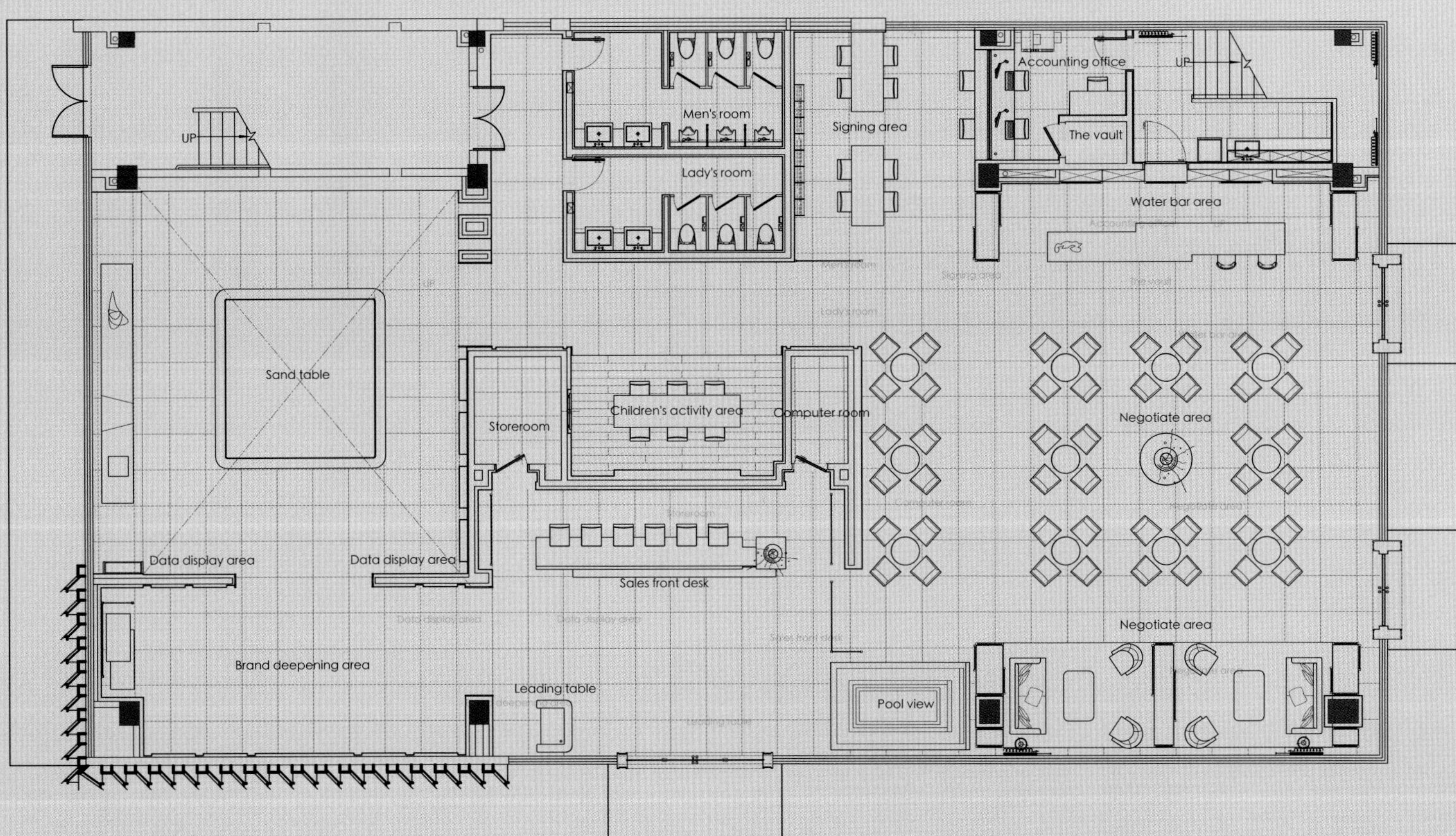

Floor plan

彩虹公馆

万直 彩虹公馆

Project:
Show House of Mattel The Masterwork

Client:
Mattel Real Estate

Location:
Huizhou

Black and White

Unity of opposites, black and white are the ultimate abstraction of colors. In this design, black, white and gray tones are used to create a chic and simple space. The space is objective yet bright, with the exuding calmness and elegance. In it, life is art and vice versa. Comfort and luxury go hand in hand to secure a simple yet personal lifestyle.

Main materials: Jobs Marble, Oak, Ceramic Tiles, Fabric, and Wallpaper
Area: 108 m^2
Design time: June 2016
Completion time: January 2017

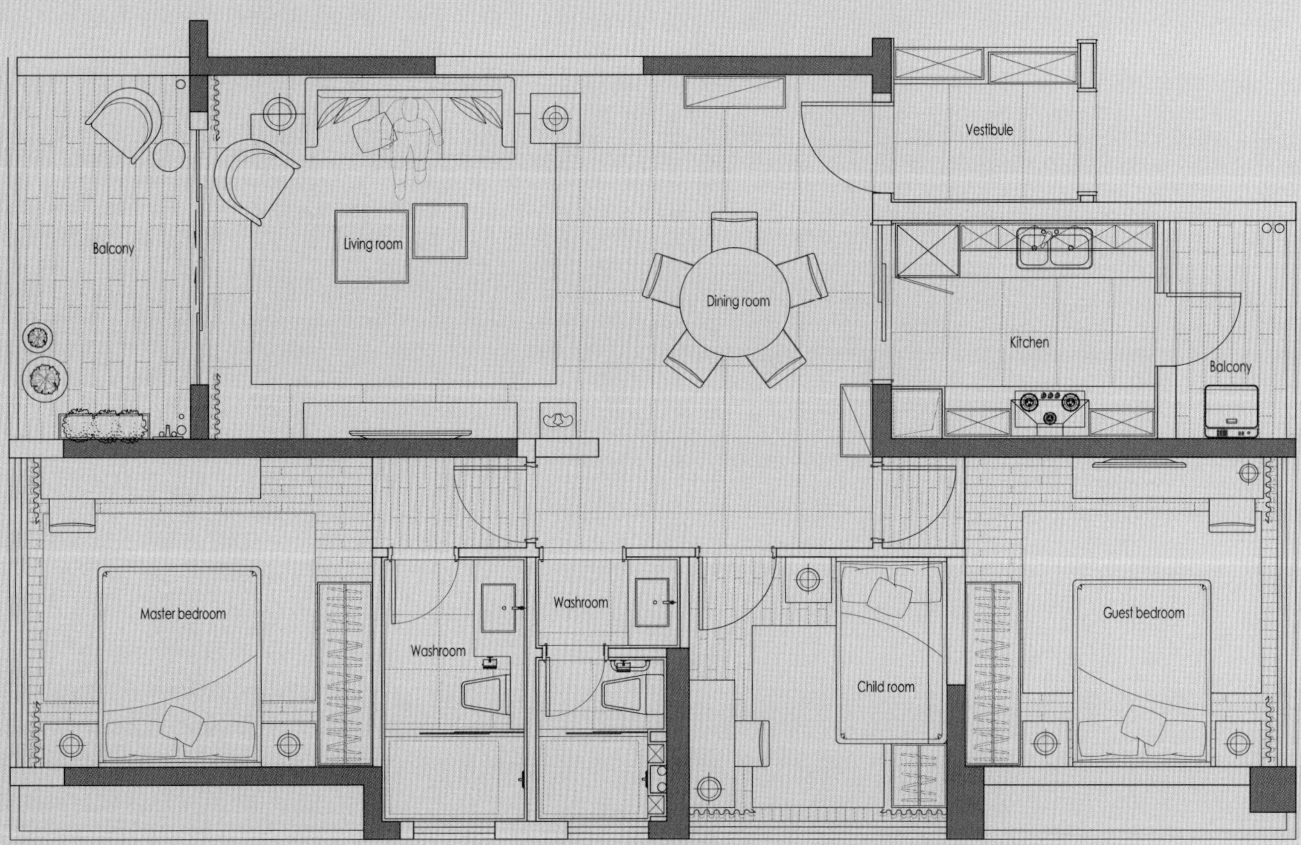

Floor plan

CORPORATE & INSTITUTIONAL

JOHN SHAW'S GUIDE TO
DIGITAL NATURE
PHOTOGRAPHY
AMPHOTO BOOKS
Berkeley
PHOTOGRAPHY

Project:
Show House of Riverside Mansion

Client:
Vincci Group

Location:
Chengdu

Colors of Autumn

As the ancient Chinese poet Lu You said, "Every year I find the autumn sunshine most charming." As autumn breeze blows, some leaves turn yellow and some red. In this design, the colors of autumn are integrated into the interior. The modern living space is interpreted with a chic yet simple approach on the theme of "nature and elegance". The light wallpaper, fish-belly white slab, and simple styling create an elegant and calm atmosphere. The exquisite and artistic furnishings add an artistic touch and the charm of life to the space.

Main materials: Paris Grey Marble, Fish-Belly White Slab, Oak, Bronze Stainless Steel, and Art Glass
Area: 137 m^2
Design time: July 2019
Completion time: December 2019

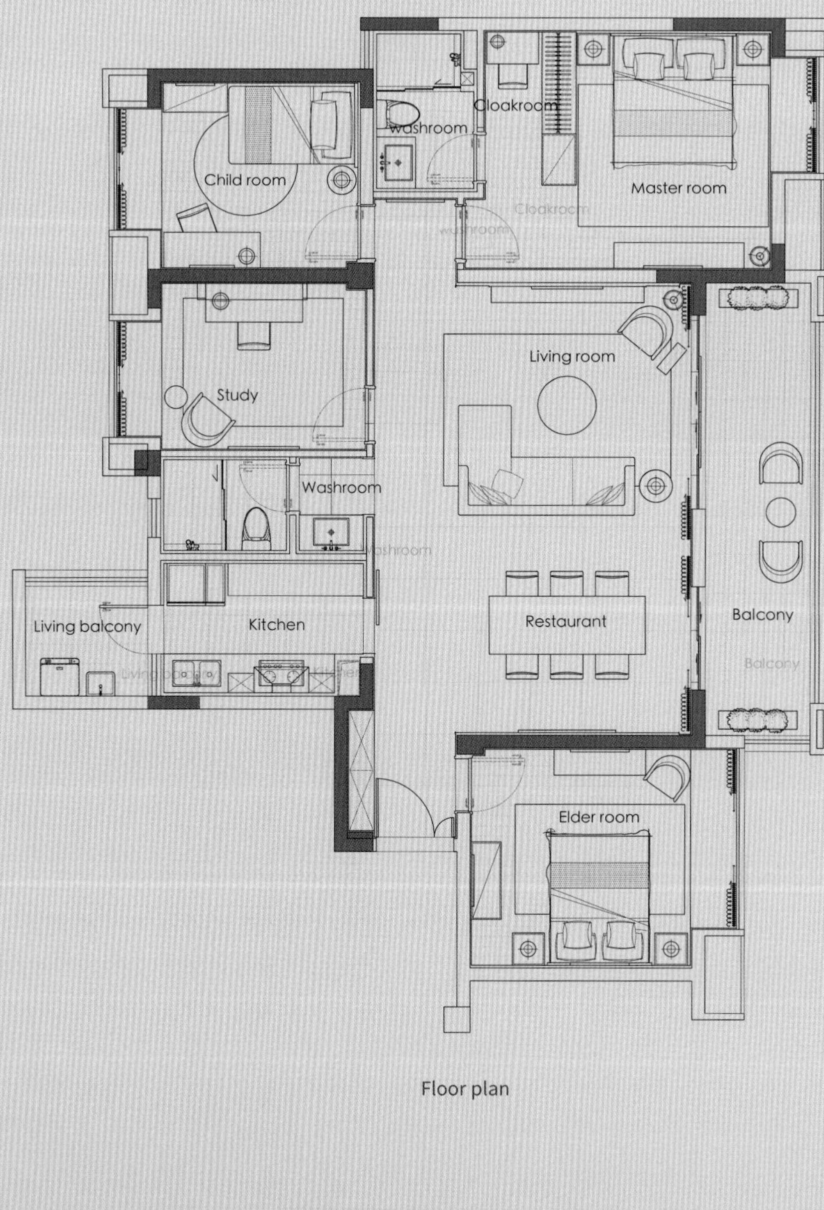

Floor plan

Project:
Show House of City Center

Client:
Aim Group

Location:
Shenzhen

Blooming Flowers

Like the blooming flowers, the space is lively and charming, filled with romance and elegance. Neoclassical furnishings are introduced into this chic yet simple space to make it modern, neat, noble yet stately. It unites the charm of sense and sensibility, offering a balance between comfort and luxury.

Main materials: Milan Gray Marble, Silver Gray Hole Marble, Burl Wood, Oak, Bronze Stainless Steel, and Art Glass
Area: 110 m^2
Design time: December 2017
Completion time: August 2019

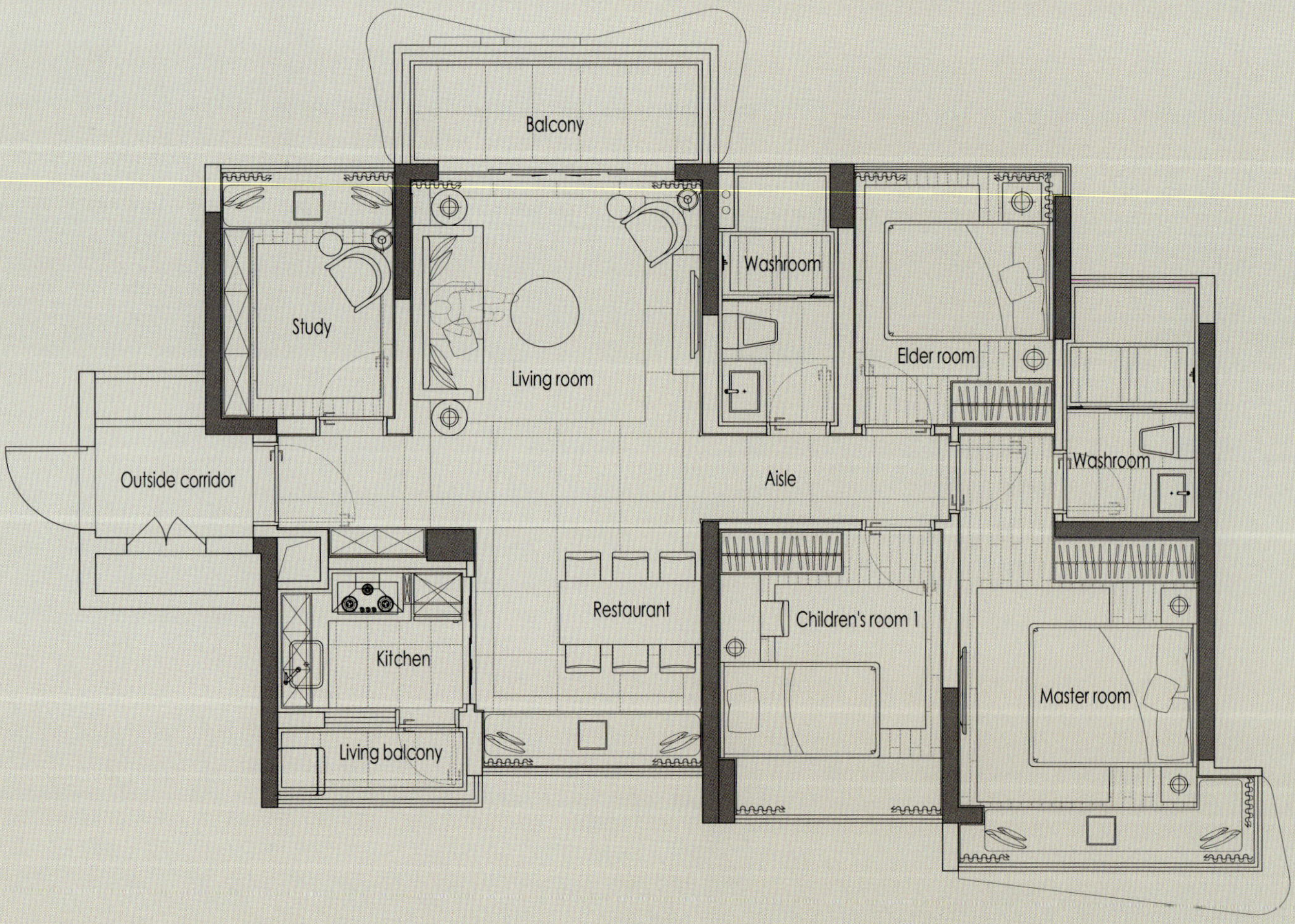

Floor plan

Project:
Show House of Tianyu Jiangpan

Client:
Hong Ding Property

Location:
Foshan

Autumn Twilight

It is pleasant to be bathed in the autumn sunshine that is slightly obscured by the thin clouds, and enjoy the beautiful scenery among mountains and rivers. As the ancient Chinese poet Han Yu sang, "Light clouds obscure the autumn sunshine and drizzles fall to the ground." In this design, the interplay between light and shadow on the French windows reproduces the scene of sunlight and tree shadows, as if the glow of a setting sun penetrates the forest. In this way, the charm of transparence and profundity emerges. Bright colors, such as beige, salmon and water blue, are combined with the calming earth tones to create an elegant and luxurious atmosphere, as well as the comfort life with Eastern aesthetics.

Main materials: Golden Jade Marble, Straight Grain White Jade Marble, Gray Alligator Juniper Wood, Black Stainless Steel, and Oak
Area: 115 m^2
Design time: October 2015
Completion time: May 2016

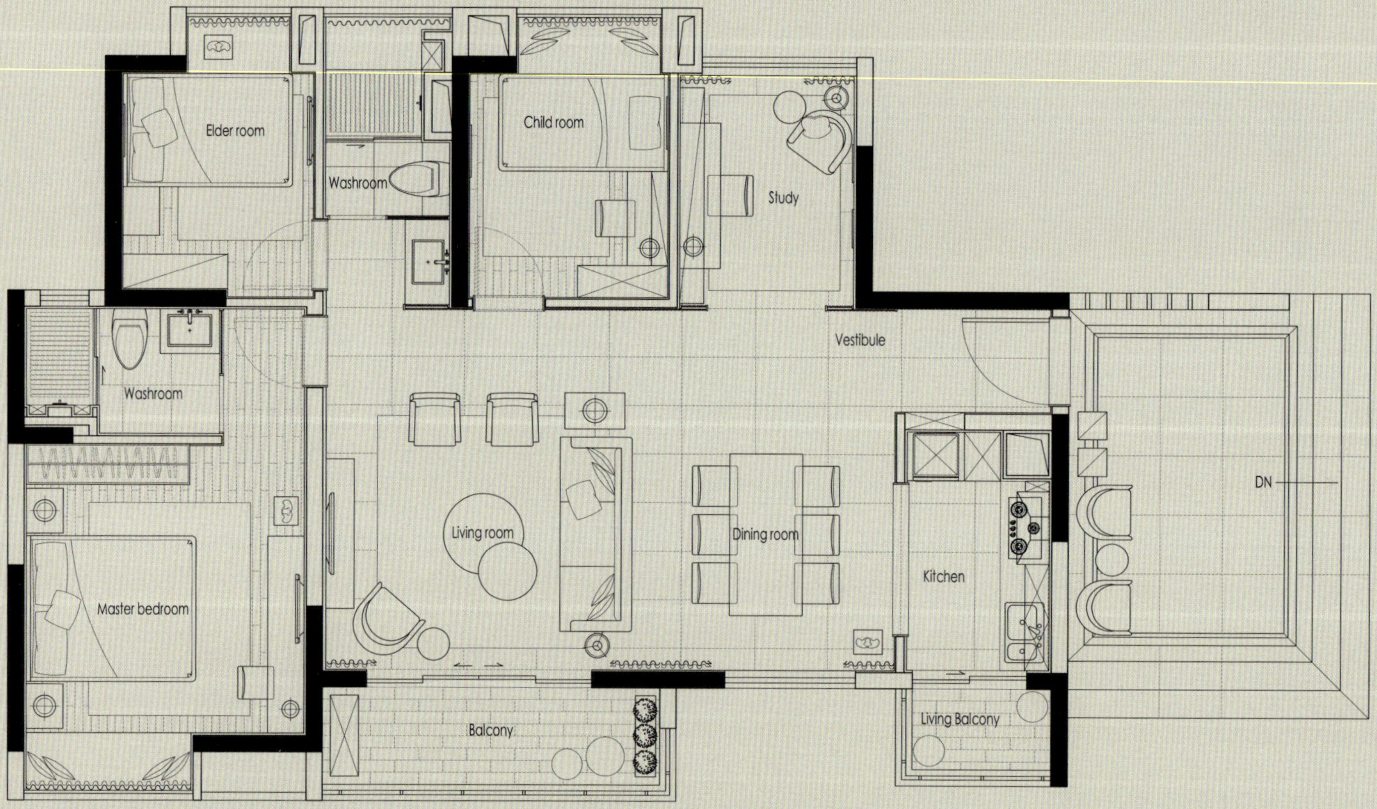

Floor plan

TOP BRAND DESIGN
CHINESE STYLE ELEGANCE

Project:
Show House of Yuerong Yuan

Client:
Kangqiao Group

Location:
Zhengzhou

Loftiness and Elegance

This design brings together a modern approach and Eastern aesthetics for loftiness and elegance. Tasteful light colors are rendered bright and vivid by different materials, creating a refreshing yet delicate space for a unique lifestyle. The designer perfects every detail of the space so that it exudes timeless charm.

Main materials: Prague Gray Marble, Oak, Wallpaper, Fabric, and Leather
Area: 260 m^2
Design time: April 2017
Completion time: March 2018

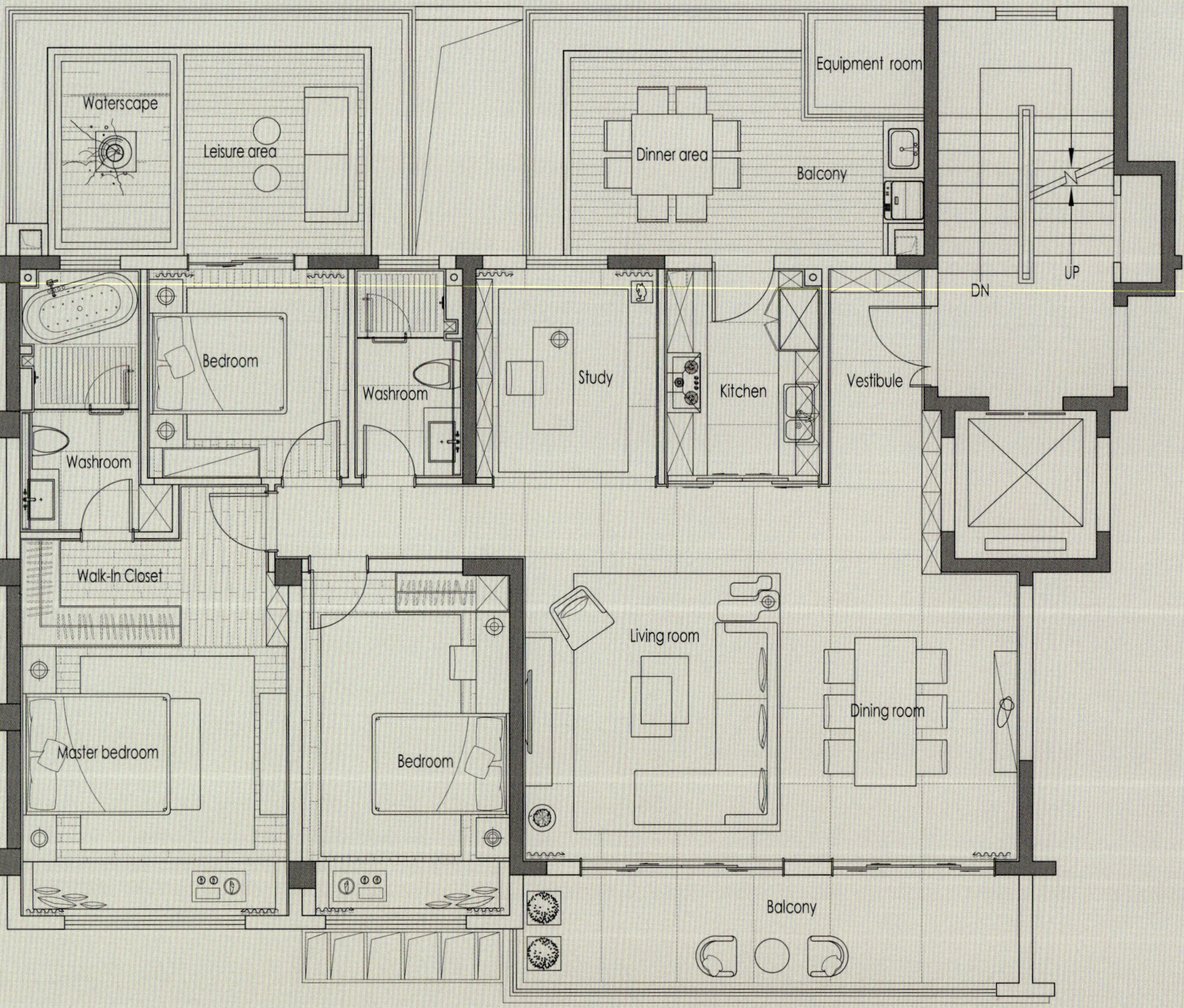

Floor plan

SUPER BOWL GOLD

Project:
Soft Furnishings for Show House of The Icon

Client:
City Mark

Location:
Shenzhen

Implicitness

The implicit is hidden. In this design, light gray tones are used to create a high-class space with well-proportioned furnishings. It is adorned by creative artistic ornaments. The interplay between light and shadow fires imagination, allowing vivid expression of every detail of the space through exquisite textures. The color palette together with the furnishings gives rise to subtlety and romance, which adds to the quality of life for future owners.

Area: 180 m^2
Design time: April 2016
Completion time: June 2016

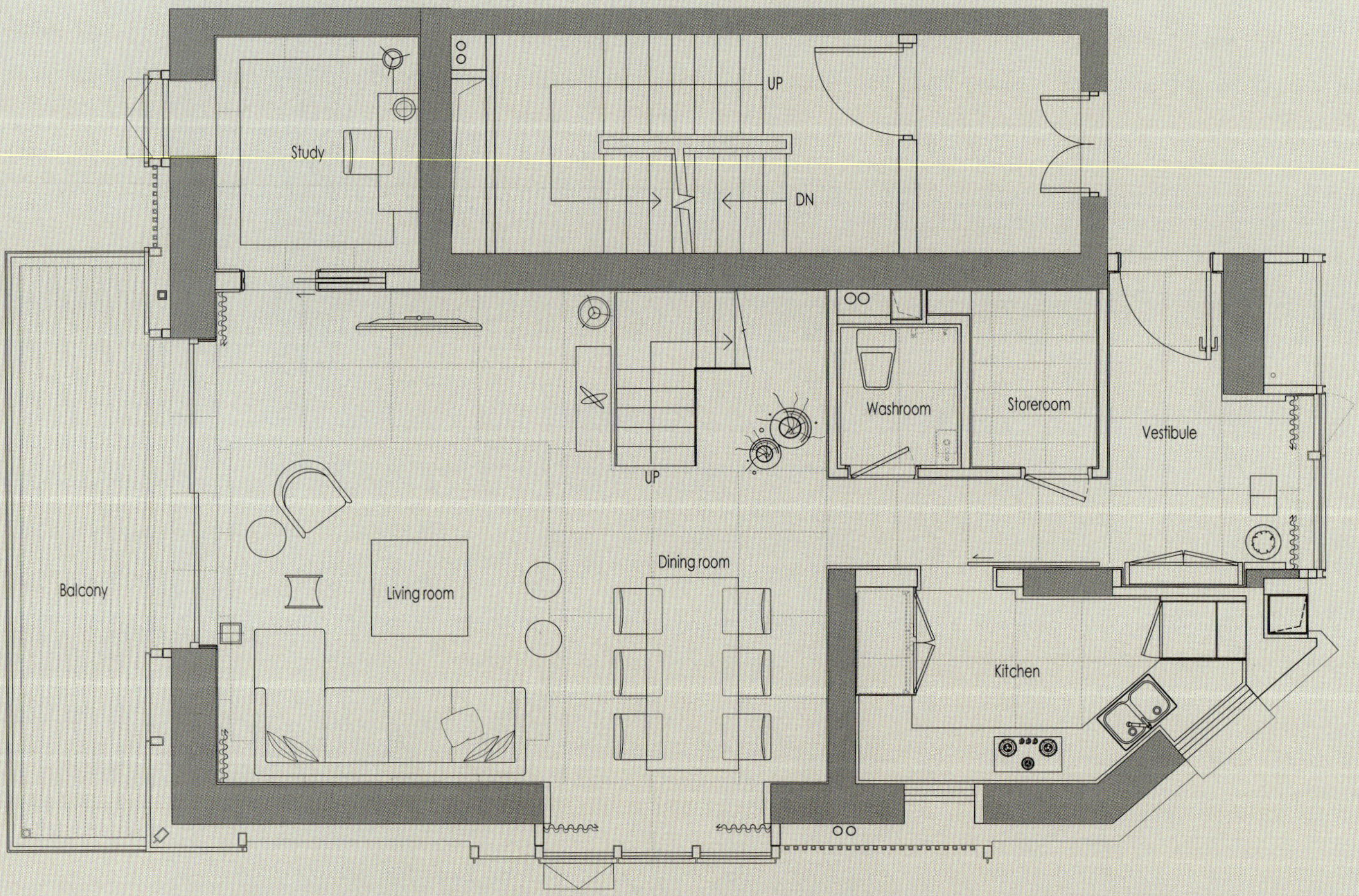

Plan of the first floor

HOTEL
HOTEL

HOTEL
HOTEL

Plan of the second floor

Project:
Soft Furnishings for Show House of The Icon

Client:
City Mark

Location:
Shenzhen

Clarity

Heidegger said to the effect that clarity allows everything to stay tranquil and intact, and that clarity is also pleasure, under whose effect everything wanders freely. Deep inside, we feel tranquil and free in this vigorous space, where imagination fired by the interplay between light and shadow, the pure and concise design aesthetics. The crafted soft furnishings together present a perfect marriage between aesthetic space and an international lifestyle.

Area: 90 m^2
Design time: June 2017
Completion time: January 2018

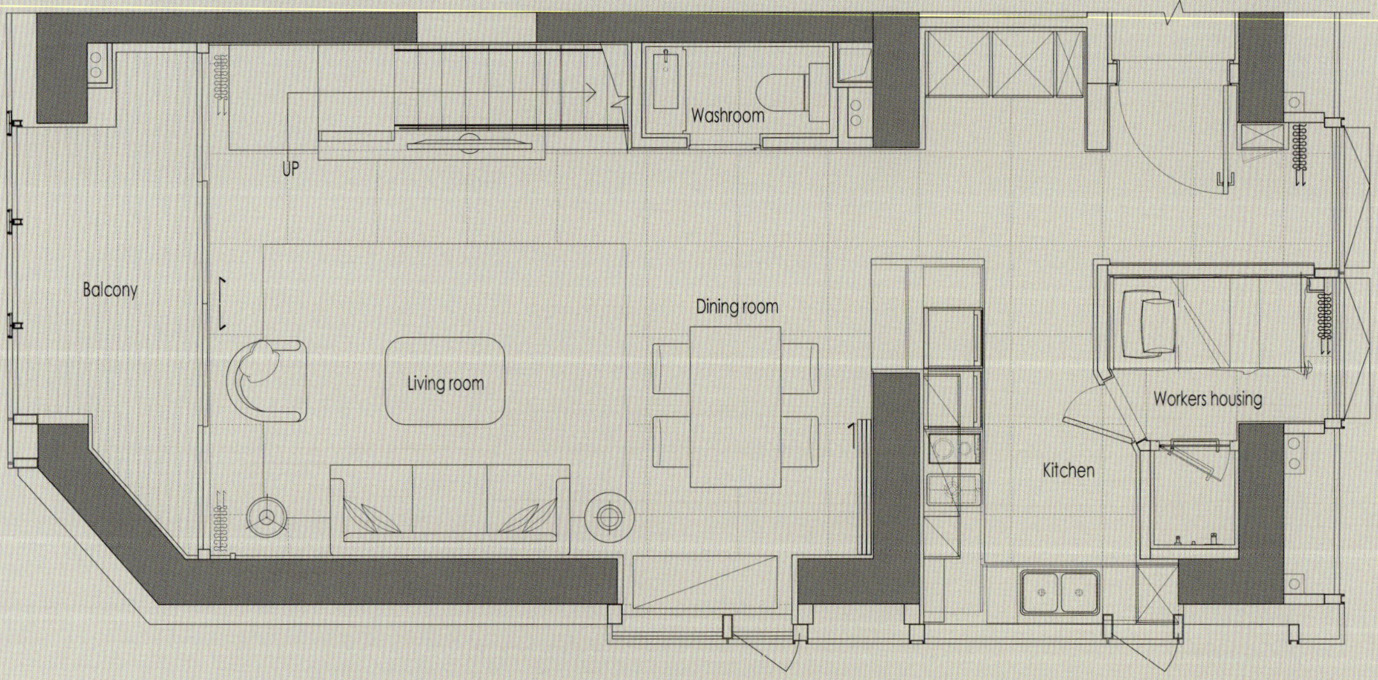

Plan of the first floor

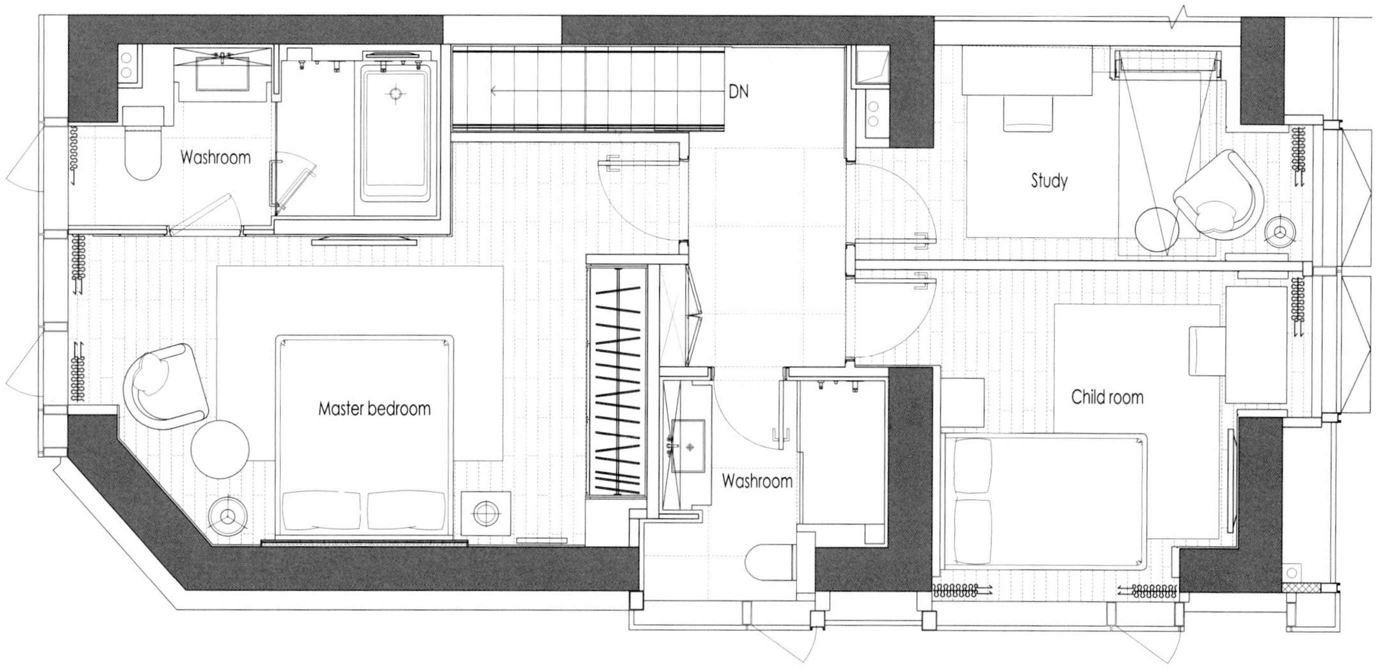

Plan of the second floor

North America Is the Lord's

Project:
Soft Furnishings for Show House of The Icon

Client:
City Mark

Location:
Shenzhen

Sharpness

In this design, soft furnishings are used to highlight a sense of sharpness, that is, the edge. The contemporary avant-garde furniture by Aston Martin is the concrete form of "gentility". Its design extends the characteristic of excellent sports cars with dynamic high-tech lines plus top-notch materials. The craftsmanship accentuates high quality, blending the trajectory of the brand with the current fashion trends to reproduce the excellence and creativity, while celebrating design heritage, and to create the future of home living.

Area: 120 m^2
Design time: June 2017
Completion time: July 2018

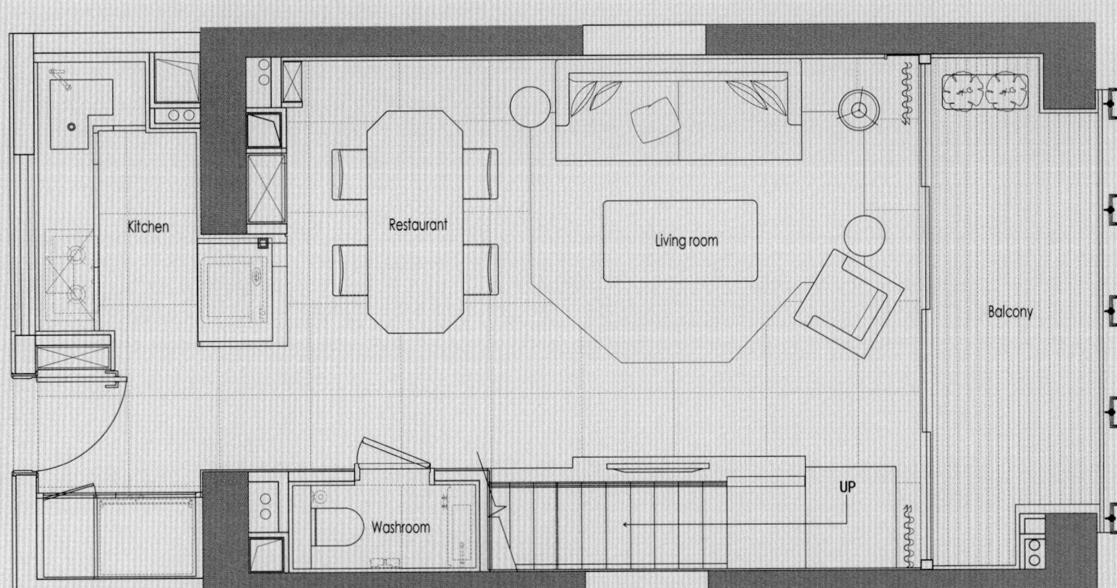

Plan of the first floor

Plan of the second floor

ASTON MARTIN
POWER, BEAUTY AND SOUL

Project:
Soft Furnishings for Villa of Bay Breeze Resort in OCT

Location:
Shenzhen

Shapeless

Located in Nanshan District, Shenzhen, this property is tranquil and elegant as it stays away from the hustle and bustle of urban life. One feels contented and comfortable in such a quiet and spotless space. As a saying goes, "Tao is plain when described with words. It is inviable and inaudible." Tao is without sound or shape. It is just like an obscure person without a gorgeous appearance. It attracts no one and will be attracted by no one. In this design, soft furnishings are creatively arranged based on the original spatial pattern to create a quiet and elegant humanistic atmosphere for a free and easy lifestyle.

Main materials: Grace Gray Marble, Snowflake White Marble, Walnut, and Latex Paint
Area: 500 m^2
Design time: July 2014
Completion time: March 2016

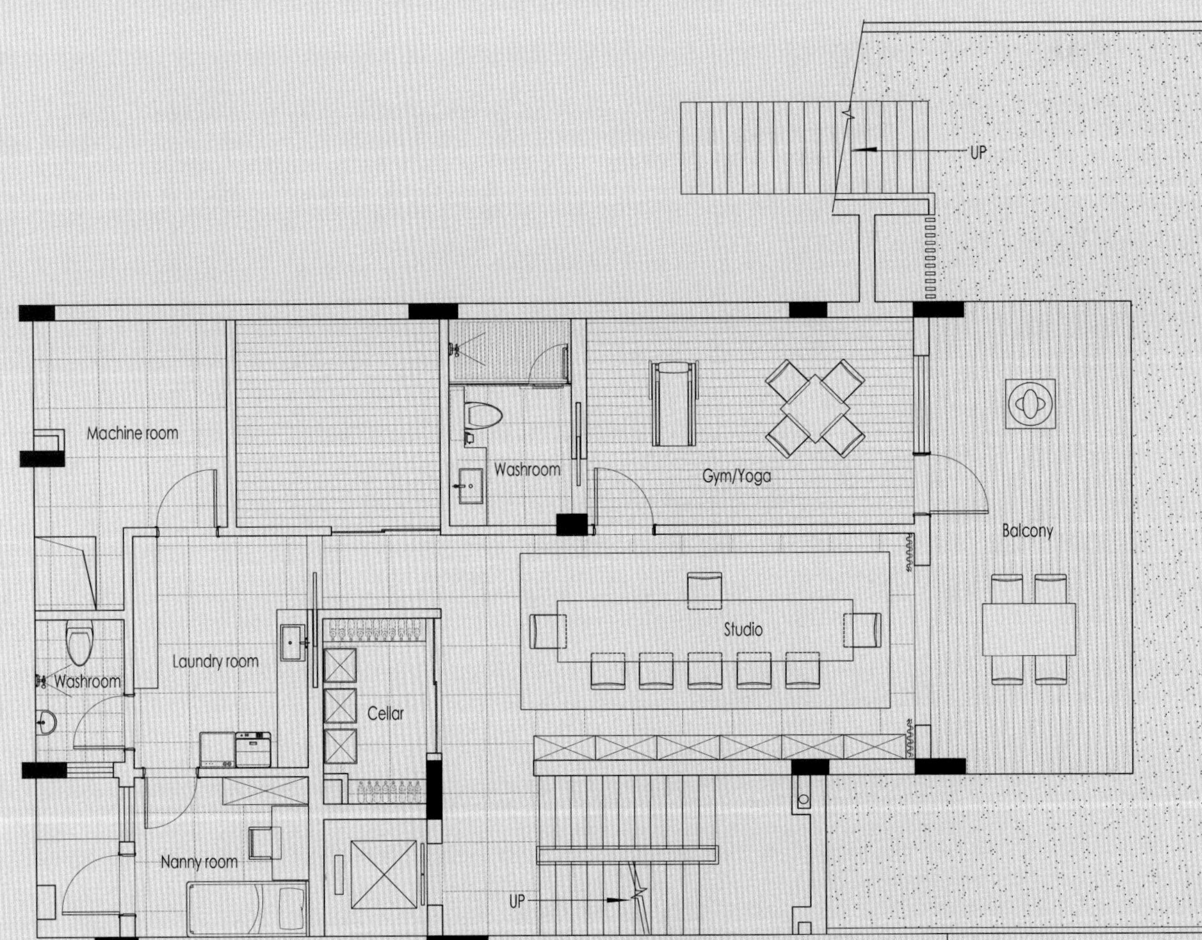

Plan of the basement

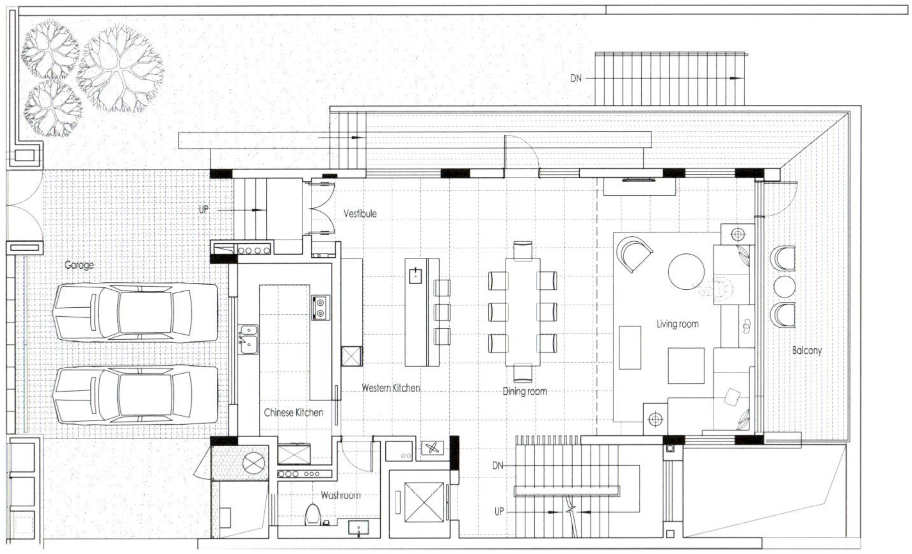

Plan of the first floor

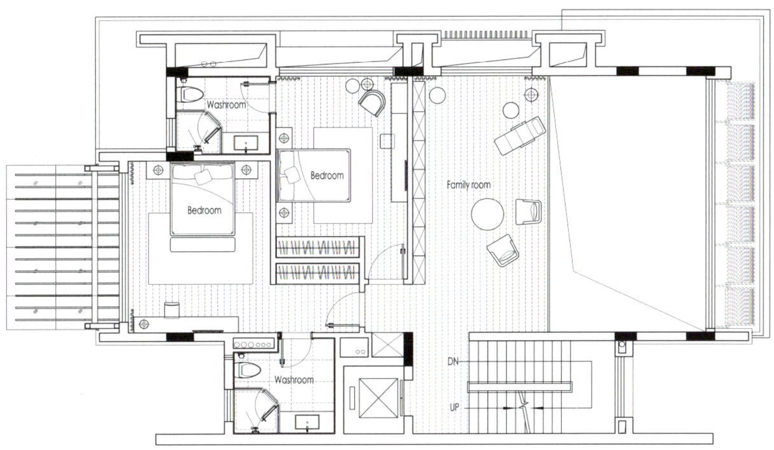

Plan of the second floor

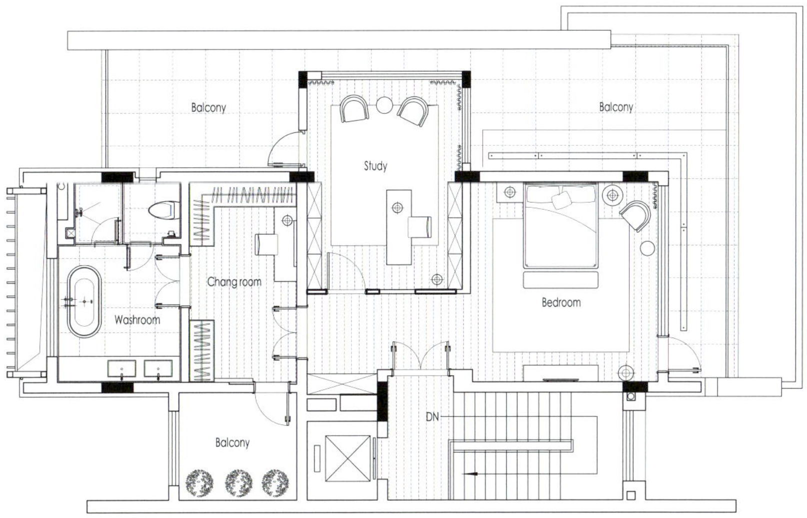

Plan of the third floor

Meier

Expo '92 Seville
Architecture and Design

East Aesthetic Design/ Refined Art Life